Embroidery & Cross Stitch

In today's hi-tech, fast-paced world, the art of embroidery and cross stitch is increasing in popularity. The range of materials, threads and patterns has never been greater. In *Embroidery & Cross Stitch* you will find an exciting range of projects including simple designs for beginners as well as more complex creations for the more experienced embroiderer.

Whether it be A Touch of Luxury, Fabulous Frame-ups, Pretty and Practical or Great to Give or Get, *Embroidery and Cross Stitch* includes projects to delight everyone. Cushions, pictures, tablecloths, samplers and even embroidered garments are featured in this comprehensive book.

Embroidery & Cross Stitch provides beautiful colour photographs, clear instructions and patterns. Mountmellick, wool embroidery, candlewicking and smocking techniques are included to delight and inspire every embroiderer.

Embroidery
& Cross Stitch

A Craftworld Book

Craftworld Books Pty Ltd
50 Silverwater Rd
Silverwater NSW 2128
Australia

First published by Craftworld Books Pty Ltd 1999

Managing Editor: Sue Aiken
Editor: Jutta Sieverding
Associate Editors: Marnie McLean, Karen Winfield
Concept: Vivien Valk Design
Designer: Claudia Balderrama
Illustrator: Annette Tamone

National Library of Australia Cataloguing-in-publication data

Embroidery & cross stitch.

Includes index
ISBN 1 876490 03 9.

1. Cross-stitch – Patterns. 2. Embroidery – Patterns.
3. Decoration and ornament. (Series: Australian Country Craft series).

746.44041

Printed by KHL Printing Co, Singapore

THE AUSTRALIAN
Country
CRAFT
SERIES
PRESENTS

Embroidery & Cross Stitch

Craftworld Books

Contents

A Touch of Luxury

Fabulous Frame-ups

Pretty and Practical

Great to Give or Get

Acknowledgments

CHRISTINE BISHOP
Schwalm Handtowel

Christine's lifetime love affair with embroidery is nothing new in her family – she's traced embroidery back through at least seven generations. She has a particular interest in old, almost forgotten stitches and techniques, among them Schwalm, for which she has produced instruction booklets. Teaching is a joy for Christine and she focuses on petit point, eyelet work, cutwork, stumpwork and, of course, Schwalm. She has also judged embroidery competitions.

VAL CALCRAFT
Beautiful Bathroom Accessories

As a child Val lived in the small New England tablelands town of Guyra, where winters were spent around the open fire with her mother and grandmothers sewing, knitting or crocheting. Val is now retired, however she still finds time for her latest needlework passion, tapestry, and is a past president of the Tapestry Guild. Always interested in art and drawing, she likes to design and paint her own canvases, then stitch over them using a variety of creative stitches and threads. Recently, Val designed a tapestry of the *Mary Rose*, King Henry VIII's salvaged warship. This complex tapestry was stitched by Val and twenty other guild members and donated to the Maritime Museum located in the heart of Sydney.

LIZ CAVANAUGH AND PAULINE THOMAS
Garden Flowers Knee Rug

Liz, a commercial artist, and Pauline, a primary school teacher, met in 1990 and formed a successful partnership built on friendship and a shared love of wool embroidery. Since then they have gone from strength to strength, producing mail order kits for cushions and blankets through their business, Liz and Pauline Design. Liz visits gardens, nurseries and florists in search of real flowers and plants for their designs, then does the initial stitching. The final patterns are stitched by both Liz and Pauline and the instructions written by Pauline. Both partners enjoy talking to customers and are happy to offer advice. New designs are constantly being added to their range.

GARY CLARKE
Purr-fectly Irresistible

A textile and design artist, Gary is quick to dispel the myth that embroidery is 'women's work'; to him it is a time-honoured artform with unlimited creative potential. His designs vary from enchanting fairies and embroidered cats to blooming flowers. 'I don't think my children are all that impressed with my work,' says Gary, who has written several books. His vision for the future also incorporates a healthier environment. To this end he makes his own paper, and recycles all his thread offcuts.

DANA COX
Smocked Summer Dress

While Dana enjoys all handcrafts, smocking is her passion. Her love affair started when on a whim, she bought a $2 smocking book on a bargain table. She prefers to use smocking as a feature as opposed to its more traditional use as a background and likes to work with bright, clean colours which often inspire the original patterns she also designs. Dana rarely adds sleeves or collars to her designs which are impractical for the warm weather Queensland always enjoys. Her work has been published in many magazines, and she teaches part-time through the Smocking Guild Qld Inc.

HELEN ERIKSSON
Antique Roses Cushion
Wool Embroidered Tea-cosy

Inspiration comes from many places for Helen – from her garden, from the work of others and from designs on cards to name but a few. She says simply, 'I like pretty things and have an eye for detail'. Helen's forte lies in design and colour. Embroidery has become a full-time career for her and she holds classes regularly.

KAYLENE EVANS
Pansy Garland

A friend first convinced Kaylene to join an embroidery group, and her passion for needlework has evolved since then. Encouraged by friends and family, she set up KAE's Treasures & Heirlooms, creating her own designs for fine embroidery and supplying kits. There is now a large number in her range, including cottage garden scenes and verses, Christmas designs, teddies and memorabilia embroidery, as well as two books. A number of Kaylene's kits feature individually handpainted backgrounds, ensuring each one is slightly different. Her aim is to design pieces that will be loved, treasured and passed on to become cherished heirlooms.

JEAN FLETCHER
Fairy Wrens in my Garden

Jean became involved in embroidery by accident – literally. A keen woodcarver and turner, she was involved in a car accident which left her unable to pursue this hobby. When a friend took her to an embroidery exhibition she was so inspired that she began taking classes. Jean went on to become a teacher of stumpwork and sells kits of her designs around the world. Much of her inspiration comes from birds and wildflowers.

PEG FRASER
Heritage Cross Stitch

Nova Scotia born Peg was taught to cross-stitch by her mother at the age of ten years. Together they worked on many projects, making up for the lack of Canadian designs by creating their own. In 1986 they started a successful partnership designing and wholesaling cross-stitch kits based on traditional Canadian themes such as quilts, hooked rugs, samplers and historic houses. Now living in Australia with her family, Peg continues to design, adding Australian themes to her repertoire. When she isn't designing, stitching or working on the restoration of the family's federation-style home, Peg can be found in the vegetable garden talking to the artichokes.

City & Guilds of London Institute examination in hand embroidery, Heather has tutored in Canada, New Zealand and the USA as well as in many parts of Australia. Her work has been shown exhibited in art galleries. Since 1988, Heather has written no less than seven books on embroidery.

JENNI KIRKHAM
The Prettiest Frame-up

This embroiderer and author is a regular contributor of projects and articles of interest to craft magazines. Jenni has also written two needlepoint books. It was while designing projects for her books that she developed her beautiful technique of creating lace effects on perforated paper. Jenni's third book includes original designs for traditional embroidery, smocking and ribbon weaving. She is currently working on her fourth book with her new designs based on a cottage garden theme.

VIVIENNE GARFORTH
Pansy Chatelaine

To quote Vivienne, she has been 'totally obsessed by crafts' since she was a small child. Vivienne's interests include tatting, dressmaking, découpage, embroidery, crocheting, collecting antique lace, linen, dolls and blue and white china. She has exhibited regularly at the Perth Royal Show, winning prizes for her embroidery, and she has written seven books. Her involvement in craft has led to numerous opportunities including demonstrating at exhibitions and conducting workshops locally, as well as at a major craft show in London. Vivienne has also been mentor to a group of embroiderers at Bandyup Women's Prison in Perth. She has now set up her own studio to give classes from home.

MERRILYN HEAZLEWOOD
Fuchsia Hot-water Bottle Cover

Merrilyn has had amazing success as a silk-ribbon embroiderer. She travels around the world, promoting her books and teaching the craft. Merrilyn's busy, professional lifestyle is a far cry from her rural childhood. Before writing and teaching full-time, Merrilyn owned three needlework shops.

HEATHER JOYNES
White Cats Needlework Set

Teacher, author and antique needlework tool collector, Heather is well-known in all of these spheres. She was one of the first members of the Embroiderers' Guild NSW Inc to successfully sit the

DEBORAH LOVE
Mountmellick Tablecloth

It was in the early 1990s that pharmacist Deborah began embroidering in earnest. Initially introduced to needlework in primary school, she attended classes with Paddy Hornsby and Diana Lampe while living in Canberra. On moving to Perth, she taught embroidery in needlework shops. Returning home to Brisbane, Deborah joined the Embroiderers' Guild Qld Inc and is their Embroiderer of the Year. While exploring whitework techniques, Deborah happened upon Mountmellick embroidery. Since then she has undertaken considerable research into the background of this 19th century technique, even visiting embroiderers in Dublin and Mountmellick when in Ireland last year.

Deborah has launched her own label, to supply kits and materials, and also teaches embroidery.

GINA MARION
Heavenly Hardanger

Gina first discovered the craft of Hardanger browsing though a book. She taught herself the technique from books, then started to change the basic shape and patterns inside it. That experimenting is just what she wants readers to do – 'The designs aren't sacrosanct,' she says. Gina's other great love is music and she points out that both her favoured embroidery technique and music, share a mathematical base. Gina teaches embroidery and has published books of hardanger designs.

JUDY SCHNEIDER
Bullion Rose Set

Judy is 64 years young, so there have been a lot of stitches sewn and a lot of bits and pieces glued and tied in that time. She has three children and four grandchildren. After years of working at a great variety of art and craft styles, she has finally found the two great loves of her life. The hand-embroidered set featured here was Judy's major work in the commercial needlecraft TAFE certificate. Her other great love is art wall quilts, which she likes to describe as painting with fabric. Judy also teaches a small weekly class in both hand and machine work.

SUE STROM
Heirloom Handkerchief Sachet

Sue's love of needlework began as a child. In fact, she says she cannot remember a time when she has not sewn. Her love of fine needlework has intensified over

the years and, after much study and the making of many garments, Sue has refined her techniques and today she concentrates on teaching heirloom sewing, smocking and fine embroidery in her home studio and other venues. Sue's classes involve lots of personal attention and are geared towards the individual needs of her students. She has produced many projects for craft and needlework magazines and has published a collection of original embroidery designs.

JOAN WATTERS
Teddy Bear Basket

Joan has been stitching since the age of five, beginning with stitching buttons onto fabric. She was trained as a dressmaker and then ran her own dressmaking business from home while her children were young, later working in retail. She is now a full-time embroidery teacher, designer and author. Through her business, Delwood Designs, Joan designs and markets kits of wool embroidered bears and blankets, as well as Brazilian and ribbon-embroidered cushions. She teaches many forms of embroidery, either in small groups at her home or in needlework shops.

RUTH WILSON
Beaded Evening Bag

Mention beads to Ruth and you'll find yourself caught up in an infectious enthusiasm. Ruth teaches dressmaking, machine embroidery and heirloom sewing as well as bead embroidery, about which she has written a book. In 1996 she completed a course at the Lesage School of Artistic Embroidery in France, and also had the opportunity to inspect beading dating back 400 years in the UK.

WENDIE YOUNG
Summer Love Baby Blanket

Initially encouraged by her mother, Wendie now has three daughters and a grand-daughter of her own, who she takes delight in embroidering for and with. Ten years ago, the owner of a local haberdashery asked Wendie to share her skills and teach a class. Since then she has expanded her knowledge, studying many forms of embroidery with highly regarded international teachers. She particularly enjoys smocking and fine embroidery, but also loves the speed of silk-ribbon work. In 1996, encouraged by her husband Colin, Wendie released her first embroidery design and has continued to add more designs to the series.

Introduction

Embroidery is one of the oldest textile crafts still in existence and is practised across the world. Its reputation as an art form has waxed and waned over the centuries, but the skill has never been lost. In today's hi-tech, fast-paced world, the art of embroidery and cross stitch is increasing in popularity. At no time in the past has the availability of materials, threads and patterns been greater. Our forebears would have been green with envy!

This book offers you many wonderful projects created by the country's leading designers and stitchers. It is suitable for both beginners and experienced embroiderers, and everyone in between. Some projects have every detail covered while others are open to interpretation so that each embroiderer's piece is truly a unique creation.

The projects are lavishly illustrated with superb colour photographs. Patterns are provided, either with the project, or if too large for the book page, then on the pull-out pattern sheet included. Many of the projects also include step-by-step diagrams to further aid the reader.

The projects were created by some of the country's most talented embroiderers, and a brief biography of each is included on the previous pages.

The projects are grouped into four sections as follows.

Exquisite embroidered items by Robyn Rich.

SECTION 4:
GREAT TO GIVE OR GET

There's nothing like a hand-made gift to let people know you care, whether it's a delightful beaded pincushion or cute name plaques for a child's room. The only problem you're likely to have is that you will fall in love with these superb projects and be unable to part with them. In addition to these projects, the book gives a brief history of embroidery and cross stitch, a comprehensive guide to the stitches used, basic equipment, transferring your design and preparing you work for framing. Settle yourself in a comfortable chair and as you select your project, remember that you are continuing a tradition that stretches back hundreds of years.

SECTION 1:
A TOUCH OF LUXURY

❖

There is nothing quite like embroidery to add a touch of luxury to garments and accessories. Whether it's the opulent touch of an embroidered cashmere wrap, or the sumptuousness of beading on a plush velvet bag. Perhaps you would prefer the delicately embroidered baby blanket, or the stunning Mountmellick tablecloth. Whatever your choice, these designs are sure to become treasured heirlooms.

SECTION 2:
FABULOUS FRAME-UPS

❖

You'll want to frame these stunning designs. And think how proud you'll feel when you tell visitors admiring a piece that you stitched it yourself! What's more, single motifs or letters from the samplers included in this section can be adapted to decorate and personalise tray mats, napkins, bookmarks, blouse pockets or anything else you can think of.

ENLARGING THE PATTERNS

Most patterns in this book need to be enlarged before use. To do this accurately, look for the photocopy symbol and number on the pattern (for example ⊟30%). Set the photocopier to the percentage given and photocopy each piece on this setting. Patterns that have the symbol ⊟SS (same size) do not need enlarging.

SECTION 3:
PRETTY AND PRACTICAL

Turn an afternoon cuppa into an elegant event with an embroidered tea-cosy and delightful old-fashioned tea cloth. Add romance and glamour to cushions. Transform a simple summer dress into something unique. Or why not pamper yourself with a needlework set that will capture the heart of any cat lover. The projects in this section all have practical applications, and will give you pleasure every time you use them.

The History of Embroidery & Cross Stitch

Practised across the world in both primitive societies and great civilisations, embroidery has flourished through the ages. The earliest known examples are Egyptian, but we know from artefacts and literature that it was also carried out in several other countries of the eastern Mediterranean region, as well as in China and India. In medieval Byzantium, court garments and religious cloths were embroidered in rich colours and ornate designs often copied from Persian models and enhanced with pearls and gold and silver threads. In medieval Greece, linen panels were embroidered in colourful silk geometric and floral patterns, influenced by Persian and Italian decorative motifs. The influence of Byzantine art has been found throughout Europe.

In Europe, embroidery developed as a means of enriching clothing, church vestments, wall-hangings and domestic linens and furnishings. The growth of the Christian church through the centuries focused a demand for ecclesiastical designs which depicted Biblical figures and saints together with the religious symbols by which they were represented. The professional embroiderers of England were acknowledged as the best in their field. Opus Anglicanum was sought after throughout the Christian world until the 15th century, when the rise of Protestant beliefs led to less ostentation in the vestments of the clergy.

The earliest embroidery to survive in England (from 906AD) is on church vestments from the tomb of St Cuthbert at Durham. The most famous British embroidery, and the largest hanging to survive the medieval period, is the 11th-century Bayeux tapestry, which is 70m (231ft) long by 49.5cm (19.5in) wide. Actually an embroidery rather than a true tapestry, it portrays in colored wool on a linen ground the events leading to the Norman conquest of England.

During the Tudor era, embroidery flourished as a domestic craft. More settled conditions after years of war led to the building of great country houses which no longer needed to be constructed as fortresses. Working furnishings for these became a major undertaking for the women of the household, and skill with a needle was seen as a necessary accomplishment for a lady. Several examples of the work of Elizabeth I and her cousin Mary Queen of Scots have survived from this period, showing a great degree of skill both in their design and technique. Clothing was also heavily embellished with patterns in various techniques, worked mostly by professional embroiderers.

Of the various styles of Spanish embroidery, the most striking was stitched on white linen with wool from black sheep. Taken to England in the 16th century, the black-on-white colour scheme developed into the popular Elizabethan blackwork.

Especially notable among the many Asian styles of embroidery were those of Iran, India, China and Japan. In 16th century India it was greatly encouraged by the Mughal emperors, under whose patronage many Persian artisans settled in India. Today, among the best-known styles are those of Kutch and Kathiawar, in which satins are stitched with floral patterns inset with pieces of reflective material.

Chinese embroidery was principally used to decorate garments. The earliest surviving examples are Tang dynasty garments from eastern Turkestan.

Especially well-known are Chinese emperors' robes, profusely adorned with traditional motifs and worked on a rich, dark ground, often black silk. One characteristic technique was void satin stitch, in which the rows of satin stitch are separated by a narrow strip of background material. Also characteristic were couched rows of silk threads covered with gold and silver. In Japan, silks continued to be embroidered with long stitches in untwisted silk threads. Flowers, birds, bold flowing lines, and abstract motifs are common.

As trade was established with India and the Far East in the 17th century, the influences of these designs were seen in European needlework. Jacobean crewel embroidery used designs based on those of Indian textiles. Worked in fine wool on wool or linen fabrics, it was used for domestic furnishings. Other decorative embroidery featured portraits and biblical scenes, often in Stumpwork, which allowed the use of padding and needlelace techniques to achieve a highly decorative, raised surface. The women who produced these pieces had usually started to develop their skills as small children, by working a series of samplers in several different techniques.

The 18th century was an age when embroidery flourished throughout the world. In the east, the silk designs of Japanese kimonos displayed an unmatched level of skill and in Europe, fashionable costume for both sexes was lavishly decorated with fine embroidery. The rich silks and brocades of the time were ideal backgrounds for finely shaded floral sprays. The discovery of new lands led to an upsurge of interest in plants and flowers, with many newly discovered species being copied from books and botanical specimens to grace the gowns of wealthy courtiers.

By the beginning of the Industrial Revolution, a simpler trend had emerged. In an age when new fabrics and

A stumpwork embroidery by Jane Nicholas, based on a 17th century design.

decorative techniques were being introduced, embroidery came to be regarded as an unsophisticated craft. However, this attitude did not prevail for long. A German printer, inspired by his wife's canvaswork designs, began to produce embroidery charts in colour which he sold throughout Europe, Britain and America with great success. Together with the brightly coloured wools from Berlin, dyed with the first chemically-based dyes to become available, the popular graph patterns started a craze for Berlin woolwork, which became one of the major embroidery techniques of the 19th century. It was used extensively on a wide range of household and personal accessories from slippers to chair covers.

The Victorians enjoyed a wide range of embroidery styles during the 19th century, including the charming samplers and elaborate alphabets which are so sought after today. White-on-white embroidery was used on underwear and household

linens, while throughout the peasant communities of Europe the traditional techniques continued to flourish. When large numbers of these people migrated to America, they took their embroideries with them, introducing new elements into the traditions of embroidery.

The popular trends of the 20th century are still around us. In the 1960s British embroiderers began an era of development which has seen the craft taken seriously in schools and colleges, and the flourishing of guilds and associations to promote the craft in many countries. The skills developed using machine embroidery and other modern techniques have seen the craft elevated to a fine art.

The continuing demand for classes, books and videos on all aspects of embroidery and cross stitch proves there are many people whose interest in this ancient craft will continue well into the next millennium.

A Touch of Luxury

There is nothing quite like embroidery to add that touch of luxury to garments and accessories. Whether its the opulence of an embroidered cashmere wrap, or the sumptuousness of beading on a plush velvet bag, embroidery adds a beautiful finish to any item. Whatever you choice, these designs are sure to become treasured heirlooms.

Cashmere Wrap & Belt

Luxuriously soft and exotically embroidered, this wrap and matching belt add an opulent touch to that special occasion. The floral and paisley design is stitched in Rajmahal Art Silks and metal thread, using six basic embroidery stitches.

PREPARATION

To prevent fraying, zigzag or overlock the edges of the cashmere. Trim the ends before fringing.

For the wrap, position the design onto the right side of fabric, lining up the vertical and horizontal lines on the design with the fabric weave. Allow about 2cm to 4cm (1in to 1³/₄in) on the sides for the turn backs. Allow 7cm to 15cm (2³/₄in to 6in) for the fringe, or as desired. Working on a hard, smooth surface, slide a sheet of carbon paper face down between the pattern and the fabric. Anchor the paper with weights. With smooth, flowing lines, trace the outline heavily with a pencil. It may be preferable to trace the design in sections.

For the belt, position the design lengthwise on the fabric, 1cm (³/₈in) from the long edge. Trace as above.

STITCHING

Follow the stitch and colour guides shown on pages 18 and 19. Use three strands of art silk and four strands of metal thread. Working with short lengths of thread is easier.

FRINGING THE WRAP

Fray both ends of the wrap, using a pin to pull away unwanted threads. Then finish the fringe as you prefer, by knotting or hem stitching. To hemstitch the fringe, use a pointed needle carrying a cream thread, pass the needle between and around approximately eight to twelve

MATERIALS

- 2m x 51cm (2¹/₅yd x 20¹/₄in) cream cashmere for wrap
- 14cm x 72cm (5¹/₂in x 28¹/₂in) cream cashmere for belt
- Rajmahal Art Silk:
  For wrap — thirteen skeins 101; eleven skeins 104; five skeins 231; six skeins 175. For belt — three skeins 101; two skeins 104; one skein each of 231, 175 and 90.
- One reel Rajmahal gold metal thread
- Tapestry needle
- Embroidery frame
- Dressmakers' carbon
- Cord for belt ties
- Buckram for stiffening belt
- Pencil
- General sewing requirements

STITCHES USED

Bullion Rose Stitch, Chain Stitch, French Knots, Satin Stitch, Buttonhole Stitch, Stem Stitch

NOTE: Some embroidery experience is required for this project, which allows the embroiderer an amount of creative licence. No two stitchers will interpret the designs in exactly the same way, making the finished product unique. It may be a good idea to experiment on a piece of scrap fabric first to find the interpretation that suits you best. The use of an embroidery frame is essential for good results. Wind silks onto a card to prevent tangling.

 HELPFUL HINT

A simple way to hand-dye Mokuba rayon ribbon is by using tea. Dip a tea bag into half a cup of boiling water until it is very strong. Soak the ribbons for three minutes or longer if you like a deeper shade, then rinse out in cold water. Press ribbons dry with a warm iron.

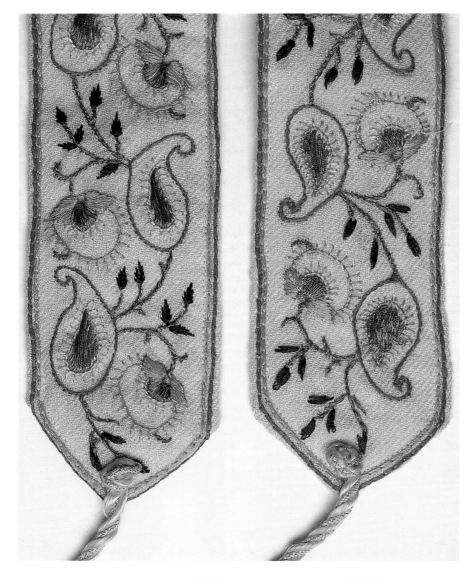

threads working from left to right, then bring the needle to the surface. Draw the thread up snugly and take a small stitch into the fell between this group of threads and the next group to the right.

To knot the fringe, take the desired number of threads between the humb and index finger of the left hand and twist them to the left. When the threads are twisted tightly, take the end of the group in the right hand and carry it up, over and through the loop formed. Work the knot up close to the fell before tightening it. An alternative is to take two equal groups of thread and simply knot them together.

FINISHING

❖

For the wrap, turn and hemstitch the sides of the wrap. Slightly dampen the wrap, place face down, cover with a thick towel and press with a warm iron. For the belt, lay buckram to the wrong side of the completed embroidery. Fold the fabric edge to edge. Top stitch the length of the belt with Art Silk 90. Cut the cord to the desired length and knot one end. Attach the other end of the cord to the inside of the belt ends and stitch securely to the wrong side before top stitching the belt ends closed. Slightly dampen the belt and press as described for the wrap.

CASHMERE BELT STITCH & COLOUR GUIDE

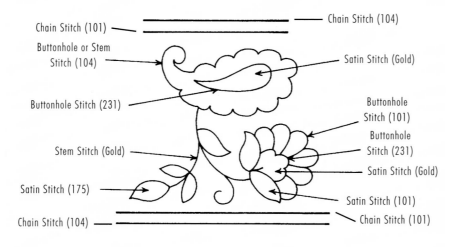

Chain Stitch (101) —
Chain Stitch (104)
Buttonhole or Stem Stitch (104)
Satin Stitch (Gold)
Buttonhole Stitch (231)
Buttonhole Stitch (101)
Buttonhole Stitch (231)
Stem Stitch (Gold)
Satin Stitch (Gold)
Satin Stitch (175)
Satin Stitch (101)
Chain Stitch (104) —
Chain Stitch (101)

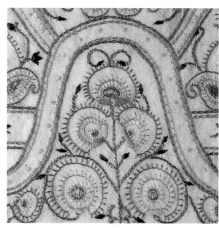

CASHMERE WRAP STITCH & COLOUR GUIDE

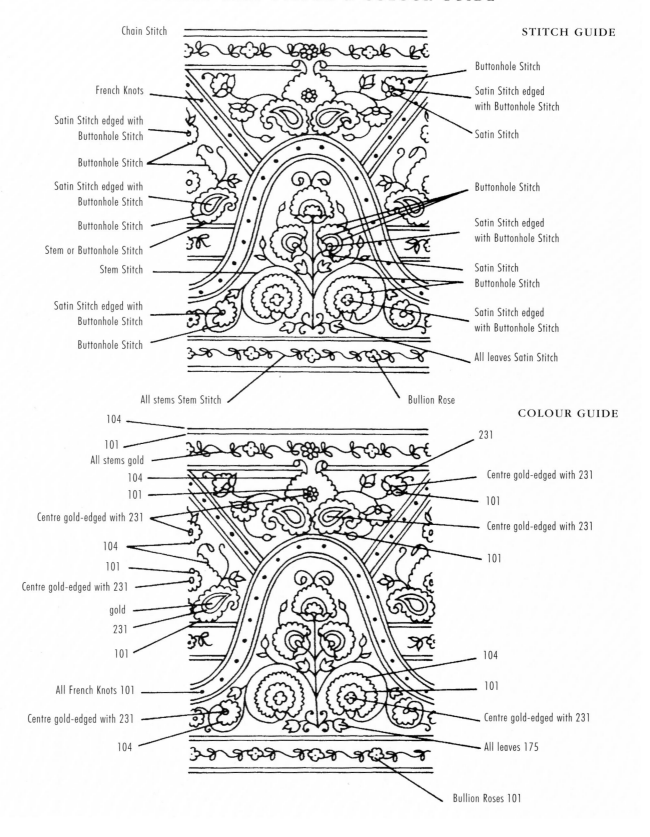

STITCH GUIDE

Chain Stitch

French Knots

Satin Stitch edged with Buttonhole Stitch

Buttonhole Stitch

Satin Stitch edged with Buttonhole Stitch

Buttonhole Stitch

Stem or Buttonhole Stitch

Stem Stitch

Satin Stitch edged with Buttonhole Stitch

Buttonhole Stitch

Buttonhole Stitch

Satin Stitch edged with Buttonhole Stitch

Satin Stitch

Buttonhole Stitch

Satin Stitch edged with Buttonhole Stitch

Satin Stitch

Buttonhole Stitch

Satin Stitch edged with Buttonhole Stitch

All leaves Satin Stitch

All stems Stem Stitch

Bullion Rose

COLOUR GUIDE

104

101

All stems gold

104

101

Centre gold-edged with 231

104

101

Centre gold-edged with 231

gold

231

101

All French Knots 101

Centre gold-edged with 231

104

231

Centre gold-edged with 231

101

Centre gold-edged with 231

101

104

101

Centre gold-edged with 231

All leaves 175

Bullion Roses 101

Beaded Evening Bag

*There's nothing quite as sumptuous and elegant as the dazzle of beads
embroidered on rich, plush velvet. Here's how to create a stunning evening bag
beaded in shades of purple, plum, amethyst and gold,
and created with raised chain stitch.*

PREPARATION

Prepare the interfacing as instructed and press onto the wrong side of the velvet. Divide the velvet into two 30cm (12in) squares. With permanent marker pen, transfer the bag outline and design, including the centre marks, from the pattern onto the sheer nylon organza. Allow to dry completely. This becomes the template. Making sure the pile will be brushing down the bag, place the template onto the wrong side of one velvet square. Pin in position, allowing at least 3cm (1¼in) on all sides.

Pressing firmly, use the chalk pencil to trace around the outline only. The shape of the bag will be indented in the pile on the right side of the velvet. Baste around this shape using contrasting coloured thread and small basting stitches. Repeat on the other velvet square.

After the outlines are basted, transfer the design onto one velvet square in the same manner.

Baste the design and the centre top and bottom marks carefully. Do not cut out. This basted outline is the finished size of the bag.

NOTE: It is helpful to practise the beading stitches on a scrap of fabric before you start on the purse. To begin, thread a double strand of cotton onto your needle. Knot the end. Come up through the fabric from the back and take a tiny stitch. This stitch secures the thread and should be used whenever beginning a new thread. Keep the line at right angles to your body and work towards yourself.

BEADING

All beading is completed before the bag is cut out and assembled.

Begin beading the outside edge using plum chunky seed beads, stitched one at a time. Bring the thread up through the velvet 1cm (⅜in) down the line from Point A. Thread one bead onto the needle, hold it in place on the line and make a stitch at the bottom of the bead, the same size as the bead, across the velvet from right to left (see Diagram 1).

Continue around the outline to within 1cm (⅜in) of Point B. Next, bead one row of raised chain stitch, beginning level with the single seed row. Bring the needle up close to the row of seed beads. Thread seven 3/cut amethyst beads onto the needle. Put the needle into the velvet, on the line at Point A on Diagram 2. Make the

MATERIALS

- 30cm x 60cm (12in x 24in) burgundy velvet (cotton velvet is best)
- 30cm x 60cm (12in x 24in) matching lining
- 30cm x 60cm (12in x 24in) Whisperweft woven fusible interfacing
- 30cm (12in) square sheer nylon organza
- 7mm x 8mm (³⁄₈in) amethyst dress stones
- 6mm x 4mm (¼in) shot purple iris centre stones
- Chunky size 8 plum seed beads, one packet
- Small size 10 3/cut amethyst seed beads, two packets
- Small size 10 light plum seed beads, two packets
- Small size 10 dark plum seed beads, two packets
- Heirloom size 14 gold seed beads, one packet
- Small quantity 2mm (⅛in) size 1 purple iris bugle beads
- Thread to match fabric and contrasting colour for basting
- 12cm (4¾in) frame
- Chalk pencil
- Permanent marker pen
- Beading needles
- Narrow edging lace (optional)
- Crewel needle
- General sewing requirements

STITCHES USED

Raised Chain Stitch

Stitch length of one bead

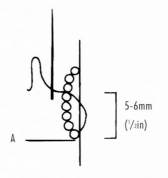

Beads should be slightly raised

5-6mm (½in)

A

Diagram 1

Diagram 2

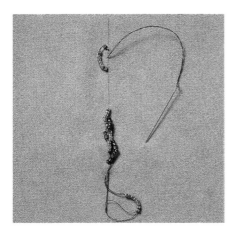

1. The light plum threads will form interlocking loops

2. Take the needle back into the velvet, two small bead widths away, around the stone. This forms a small loop of seed.

length of the stitch slightly shorter than the length of the beads so that the loop of beads is slightly raised. Bring the needle back up 5-6mm (^{1}/$_2$in) along the line, to the right of the row of beads.

Thread eight light plum beads onto the needle. Put the needle into the velvet at Point B and come back up at Point A, to the right of the row of beads (see Diagram 3). The beads will form interlocking loops as shown in the step 1 photograph (top left).

Repeat this, always coming back up on the same side, alternating the colours and finishing level with the seed bead row.

Dot small gold seed beads at approximately 1cm (^{3}/$_8$in) intervals beside the raised chain row.

Repeat this border on the second piece of velvet for the back of the bag.

Begin beading the design by attaching the 8mm (^{3}/$_8$in) dress stones in the positions marked with a large circle on the design. It is best to use a small seed bead in a matching colour to cover the hole on the dress stone. Bring the thread up through the velvet and through one hole in the stone. Thread a seed bead onto the needle and pass the needle back into the same hole in the stone. Secure the thread at the back and repeat for the other hole. The seed bead forms an anchor to hold the bead down.

Bead around this stone with groups of three gold heirloom beads. Bring the thread up beside the stone. Thread three gold beads onto the needle, then take the needle back into the velvet, two small bead widths away, around the stone. This will form a small loop of seeds. Repeat these loops to surround each of the dress stones. Refer to the step 2 photograph below left.

Next, attach the 4mm (^{1}/$_4$in) centre stones in the positions marked with a small circle on the design. Take a stitch the same size as the bead and sew through the bead twice to secure. Bring the thread up beside the stone at Point A. Thread up six small gold beads onto the needle and position them around the bead to Point B. They should only go halfway around. Take a stitch in at the last bead and come up on the other side of the stone at Point A. Thread enough small seed beads onto the needle to wrap around to the other side. The beads should fit neatly around the central larger bead as in Diagram 4. Complete all six centre stones in this way.

Once the dress and centre stones are in place, the joining sprays may then be beaded. Begin with the central stem, using single 3/cut amethyst seeds one at a time, as you did for the border.

Attach a loop of 3/cut amethyst seeds

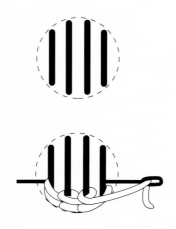

Raised Chain Stitch

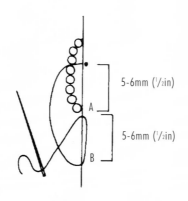

5-6mm (^{1}/$_2$in)

5-6mm (^{1}/$_2$in)

A

B

Diagram 3

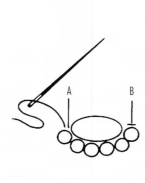

A   B

Diagram 4

for each leaf, as follows. Bring the needle up at the stem end of the leaf position (represented by the longer line on the design). Thread up enough seeds to form a loop to equal the length of the leaf. Lay the beads along the line and take a small stitch at the tip of the leaf. When all the leaves are attached, place two small bugle beads in the same way at each leaf junction (represented by the shorter line).

By the same method, attach the dark plum seeds in the positions marked beside the dress stones.

Referring to the step 2 photograph on page 22, sprinkle the gold single seeds and groups of three seeds in position.

MAKING UP

❖

Cut the lining into two 30cm (12in) squares. Transfer the outline only of the purse onto both sections, using the template as before. Lay the lining, tracing-side up, over the right side of the fabric. Match the up centre top, centre border and corners. Pin and baste across the top section marked with a dotted line on the pattern. Sew along the line using small stitches on a sewing machine. Trim the seam to 4mm (1/8in) and clip into the corners. Repeat for both front and back. Refer to the photograph of Steps 1 and 2. Turn to the right side and press carefully. Cut out the lining sections, allowing a 1cm (3/8in) seam. See the photograph of Step 3. Pin front and back lining sections, right sides together, making sure to match Points A and B. Sew the lining together, beginning at Point A and tapering in to a 1.5cm (5/8in) seam allowance. This will ensure that the lining does not interfere with the edging and sits flat inside your purse. Trim the seam to 5mm (3/8in). Trim the velvet front section, leaving a 1.5cm (5/8in) seam allowance around the beaded border.

Fold the seam allowance under neatly beside the single seed border.

Pin and baste in place. See the photograph of Steps 4, 5 and 6. Repeat for back.

Pin and baste front to back, matching the corners. To join the two sides of the bag together, use dark plum seeds and a beaded edging stitch. Begin at Point A, taking a few small stitches to secure the thread. Sew one bead onto the edge, taking a little stitch across both edges, and working from the back to the front. Pass the needle back through the loop attaching the bead and pull firmly. Thread another bead onto the needle and repeat. By looping the thread around each time, you straighten the bead and make it secure.

ATTACHING THE FRAME

❖

Position the top of the bag inside the frame matching the centres.

To hold the frame in place while you attach it, first baste roughly over the top of the frame and into the fabric (not through the holes). Then thread a crewel needle with four thicknesses of thread in a colour to match the fabric. Begin near the hinge side of the frame and secure the thread by taking a few small stitches. Sew on both sides of the frame, making two stitches into every hole, passing the thread across the back on the inside top section of the bag. To finish the bag at the corners below the hinge, simply tuck in the edge of the bag, approximately 2cm (3/4in) down on each side.

If you wish, you may gather a piece of narrow lace and stitch or glue it inside the top edge of the handle to cover the stitches on the lining.

Finally, remove all basting thread carefully from the bag, including any thread visible behind the beaded design.

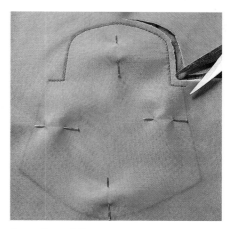

Steps 1 and 2

Step 3

Steps 4, 5 and 6

BEADED EVENING BAG
Design Outline

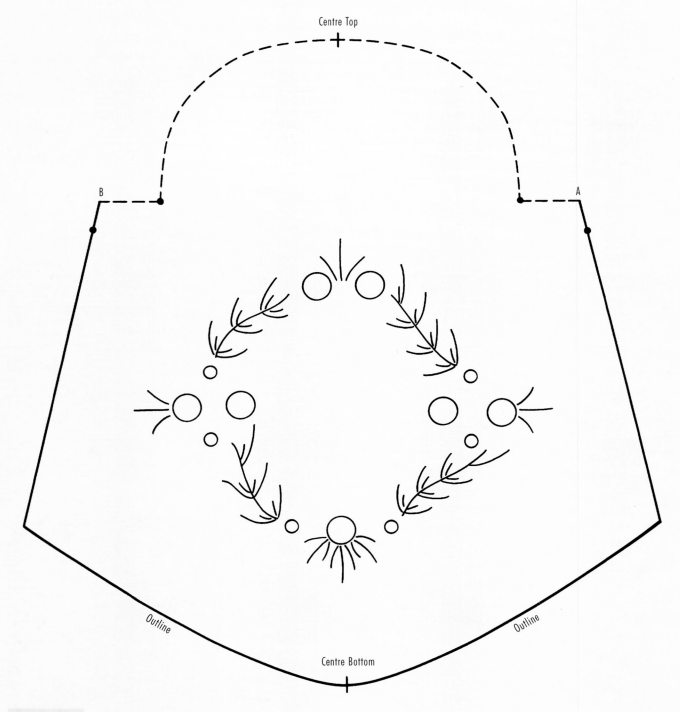

127%

Summer Love Baby Blanket

*A flock of the happiest bluebirds flutter
around a bullion rose wreath in this exquisite design.
The summerweight wool blanketing is
stitched in hand-dyed Gumnut Yarn pure silk thread.*

FINISHED SIZE

• 75cm x 110cm (29^1/$_2$in x 43^1/$_2$in)

MATERIALS

• 75cm x 110cm (29^1/$_2$in x 43^1/$_2$in) wool flannel

• Gumnut Yarn Buds pure silk thread: one skein each of pale pink (073), medium pink (075), blue (389), light green, (675), medium green (677), dark green (679), off-white (991)

• YLI silk floss: one skein of black (800)

• No 20 chenille needle

• No 1 straw needle

• Scissors

• Tape measure

• Water-soluble felt-tip pen

• 75cm x 110cm (29^1/$_2$in x 43^1/$_2$in) backing fabric (optional)

• 4.25m (4^5/$_8$yd) blanket binding

STITCHES USED

Stem Stitch (thread-up),
Bullion Rose Stitch, Straight Stitch,
Satin Stitch, French Knot, Fly Stitch

PREPARATION

Photocopy the design on page 29 at 128%. (Trace the design from the pattern onto paper.)

Place the design and blanket over a light box, with the design in the middle of the blanket and trace the design with a water-soluble pen. If a light box is not available, make a transfer using a transfer pencil and tracing paper, then heat-set it onto the blanket.

EMBROIDERY

Begin with dark green (679) in a No 20 chenille needle and work the stems and vines in Stem Stitch (thread-up).

Next work the bullion roses (see below) using a No 1 straw needle and pale pink (073) for the two nine-wrap inner bullions, and medium pink (075) for the five 12-wrap outer bullions.

The rosebuds are two nine-wrap inner bullions in pale pink (073) with a 12-wrap bullion on either side in medium

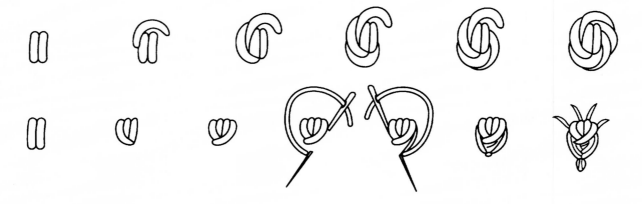

Bullion Rose Stitch

Detail of bluebirds and bullion rose wreath.

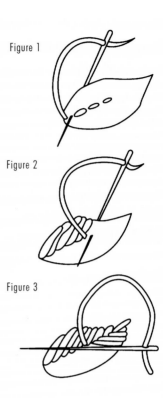

Diagram 1

Figure 1

Figure 2

Figure 3

Diagram 2

pink (075). Refer to Diagram 1. With dark green (679) in No 20 chenille needle, add four to five straight stitches on either side of the bud and three to four tiny straight stitches into the same holes to form the calyx. Then work a Straight Stitch for the stem. Finish the rosebud with three or four small Straight Stitches from the top of the bud.

Add the Satin Stitch leaves using a No 20 chenille needle and green threads (675, 677 and 679). See Diagram 1.

Finally, stitch the bluebirds. See Diagrams 2 and 3. No matter how hard you try, no two bluebirds are ever quite the same; each develops its own distinct personality.

Use a No 20 chenille needle throughout. Start your thread with running stitches rather than a knot. End threads by weaving through the back of previous stitches. Where you need a crisp, clean line, take the needle down into the fabric on that line. To create a ridge (as at the chin line), take your needle down into the holes used for previous stitches. To get a smooth line between two colours (as between bib and underbelly), bring the needle out just grabbing the edge of the previous stitch, splitting the thread.

STEP-BY-STEP STITCHING OF THE BLUEBIRD

1.

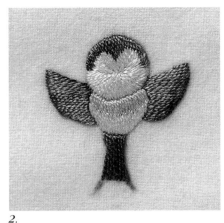

2.

3.

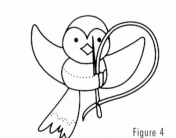

Figure 4

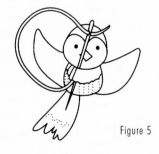

Figure 5

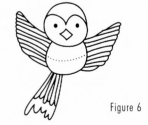

Figure 6

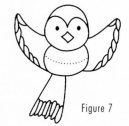

Figure 7

Using Diagram 3 as a reference, start with the face (figure 1). Use off white (991). Do not knot the thread, but make a couple of tiny running stitches then bring the needle out at the centre. With the thread up, insert the needle into the outside line of the face, coming up again near the centre.

Work Satin Stitches around the face in a clockwise direction (figure 2). Tiny wedge stitches will need to be used to fill in the circular face. This will also avoid a large hole forming in the middle.

Satin stitch the head with blue (389). Bring the needle out just grabbing the edge of the white face stitches, then insert the needle into the outside line (figure 3).

Following the steps in Diagram 4, work the underbelly in off white (991). Bring the needle up at the edge of the bib line, then stitch down into the lower edge (figure 4).

Satin stitch the bib in pale pink (073). Bring the needle up to grab the top edge

of the underbelly, then stitch down into the chin, forming a ridge (figure 5).

The wings and tail are satin stitched in blue (389). Use wedge stitches if you need to help define the shape (figure 6).

Using off white (991), stem stitch the wing tip and straight stitch the tail tip (figure 7).

With six strands of black YLI silk, work French knot eyes, a straight stitch beak and fly stitch feet.

MAKING UP

If you wish to launder your blanket before making up, handwash in pure soap. Rinse well, remove excess water and lay flat to dry. Do not tumble dry. Press the embroidery from the back with a warm iron. If using a backing fabric, baste it to the blanket before stitching the binding around the edges, mitring the corners.

Diagram 3

SUMMER LOVE BABY BLANKET
Design Outline

125%

Smocked Baby Nightgown

This charming nightie is the perfect gift for a newborn baby.
The Grace L Knott pattern has been smocked
at the front and on the sleeves in a
delicate design using cream and green threads.

PREPARATION

Following the pattern layout, cut out the garment. Pin and sew the under arm and side seams.

The pattern suggests pleating nine rows on the front, two rows on the backs, as well as top and bottom of the sleeves. This is optional as the backs and sleeve tops may be gathered, so that only the front and the cuff edge of the sleeve are smocked (as in our example).

If using smocking dots, apply to the wrong side of the fabric. Alternatively, you might choose to have your fabric pleated by a smocking machine. Pleat nine full-space rows (including holding rows) on the nightie front. Tie off the pleating threads to measure 23cm (9in). If you are machine pleating, unpick six pleats on each side of the sleeve. Tie off pleating threads to measure 10cm (4in).

SMOCKING

Refer to the graph and stitch guide shown on page 32.

Rows 1 and 9 are holding rows. On Row 1, work a row of outline stitch in cream and a row of stem stitch in green.

Starting from the centre pleat in Row 2, work two-step trellis to the right. Turn the fabric upside down and complete the row, working again to the right.

Continue working the two-step trellis according to the graph. On Rows 7 and 8, work five-step trellis.

You may choose to work double flowerettes in green where shown on the graph or, alternatively, work bullion roses if you prefer.

For the sleeves, work two rows of two-step trellis in cream thread to form a diamond pattern.

Again, work double flowerettes or bullion roses as you prefer.

Continue to make up according to the pattern. Remove pleating threads after the nightie has been completed.

MATERIALS

- 92cm x 115cm (36in x 45in) Imperial batiste
- Grace Knott Baby Nightie (newborn size)
- Edmar Iris thread: one skein each of cream and green (or the colours of your choice)
- No 8 crewel needle
- Three press studs or small buttons to fasten back opening
- Smocking dots (optional)

STITCHES USED

Outline Stitch, Stem Stitch, Double Flowerette, Two-Step Trellis, Five-Step Trellis

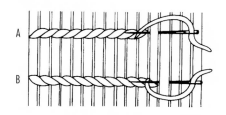

Diagram 1
A: Outline Stitch
B: Stem Stitch

SMOCKED BABY NIGHTGOWN

Graph

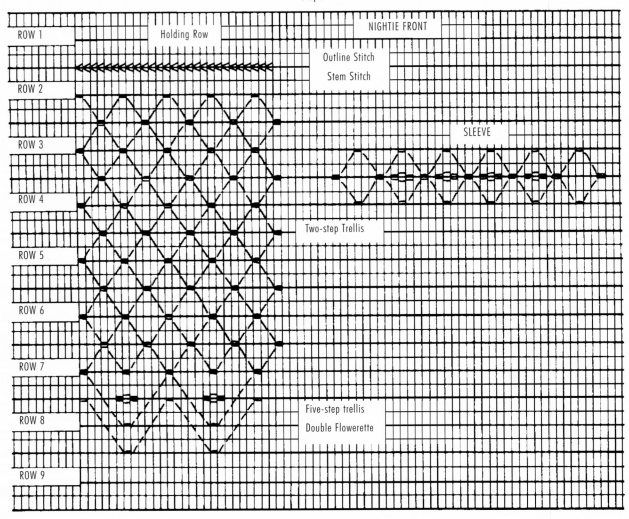

ROW 1 — Holding Row — NIGHTIE FRONT

Outline Stitch
Stem Stitch

ROW 2

ROW 3 — SLEEVE

ROW 4 — Two-step Trellis

ROW 5

ROW 6

ROW 7

Five-step trellis
Double Flowerette

ROW 8

ROW 9

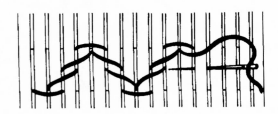

Two-Step Trellis
(Trellis down thread up)

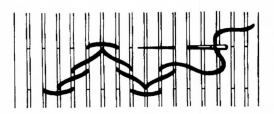

Two-Step Trellis
(Trellis up thread down)

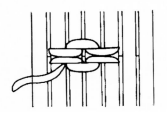

Double Flowerette

Heirloom Handkerchief Sachet

This elegant sachet embroidered in soft pastel threads
is sure to become a treasured keepsake.
It uses a variety of embroidery stitches and is trimmed
with handmade twisted cord and tassels.

MATERIALS

- 30cm (12in) Swiss cotton voile or similar fabric
- 30cm (12in) batiste for lining
- 44cm x 27cm (17³/₈in x 10⁴/₅in) Pellon
- No 50 Gütermann white cotton machine thread
- DMC Stranded Embroidery Cotton: one skein each of apricot (950), bright apricot (3779), pale blue (775), deeper blue (932), yellow (677), deeper yellow (676), pale yellow (746), green (524), grey (318)
- No 3 DMC Coton Perlé in white (for tassel)
- Mill Hill glass seed beads No 02010 for tassel (optional)
- DMC Stranded Embroidery Cotton in white (for tassel optional)
- Thick cardboard
- Straw needles No 10 and No 8
- 2B pencil
- Sticky tape
- Embroidery hoop
- 140cm (55in) mini piping in white
- 6cm (2²/₅in) wide strip of sturdy cardboard
- General sewing requirements

STITCHES USED

Shadow Stitch, Satin Stitch, Lazy Daisy (Detached Chain) Stitch, Fly Stitch, Bullion Lazy Daisy Stitch, French Knots, Bullion Rose Stitch, Split Stitch

Bullion Lazy Daisy Stitch

PREPARATION

Read all the preparation notes before cutting the voile.

The required size of the voile for the sachet is 44cm x 27cm (17³/₈in x 10³/₄in). To ensure your fabric is on the grain, withdraw a thread horizontally and then vertically and cut along the lines created.

NOTE: If you are using an embroidery hoop, it will be necessary to work with a piece larger than the required size until the embroidery is finished. Draw the threads to mark the appropriate measurement but do not cut until the embroidery is complete.

Fold the fabric in half across the narrowest width and press the fold line. Pull the fabric in to shape if the grain lines are out. Open out the fabric and place it over the design given on the Pattern Sheet, positioning the fold line where indicated. Pin the voile to the design so it will not move and lightly trace the design lines with the 2B pencil. Take particular care to transfer all the dots for the centre lattice area as accurately as possible.

EMBROIDERY

Do not use knots to commence a thread, but leave a tail hanging and fasten off later. If you are not using an embroidery hoop, care must be taken to stretch the fabric between the fingers as each stitch is pulled up.

DAISIES

See the front right corner of the design on the opposite page and follow the colour code on the pattern sheet for the placement of each coloured flower.

Using a No 10 straw needle threaded with one strand of cotton, satin stitch each petal twelve times over into the same holes. Lay the threads as you go, so that each petal is rounded and smooth. Stitch flowers A in apricot, B in blue, Y in yellow. Still using the straw needle and a single strand of cotton (flowers A in bright apricot, B in deeper blue, Y in deeper yellow), form an open lazy daisy stitch around each petal, coming up and down just short of the base of the petal. If you go right to the base, the stitch will tend to slip up onto the petal.

The daisy centres are five or six French knots (two-wraps) worked in one strand of green thread. The knots can spill over between the petals.

BULLION BUDS

Thread a No 8 straw needle with two strands of cotton and work the bullion stitch with 20 wraps as in the diagram below. Surround the bud with a fly stitch in one strand of green. Work four small single satin stitches in green around the top of the bud, as shown on pattern.

STEMS

Work all stems in split stitch. This is similar to a back stitch except the needle pierces the previous stitch. Use a No 10 straw needle and one strand of green thread.

LEAVES

Using one strand of green and a No 10 straw needle, work 12 satin stitches into the same hole in the same manner as for daisy petals. Shadow stitch the area around the centre design with two strands of grey thread in the No 8 straw needle.

With a pressing cloth, iron the embroidery on the wrong side, ensuring that the work is free of any puckers. Position the embroidered piece over the Pellon rectangle whith the right side facing upwards. Carefully baste the two layers together with machine thread, avoiding the centre latticed area.

FRENCH KNOTS

Using two strands of grey thread in the No 8 straw needle, work two-wrap French knots over all dots on the design. Take care to keep them straight and evenly placed. The knots are worked through both the voile and the Pellon to give a slightly quilted effect. On completion of the knots, lightly press down on the wrong side of the embroidery again using a cool iron and a pressing cloth.

MAKING UP

If you have been working the embroidery on a piece of fabric larger than the required size, cut away the excess voile. Trim the Pellon if necessary.

With right sides together and piping facing inwards, machine-stitch the piping around the voile padded rectangle, using the broken lines on the pattern design as a guide. Leave 1cm ($^3/_8$in) of piping unattached at the beginning. Start and finish the stitching on one of the sides of the sachet back, keeping the stitching as close to the piping as possible. Use the zipper foot on your sewing machine.

Round off the corners, then clip the fabric seam allowance of the piping nearly up to the machine stitching (at the corners only).

Machine-stitch almost to the beginning of the piping. Cut off any excess piping, leaving a 3cm ($1^1/_4$in) tail. Remove a piece of the cord from inside the fabric of the 3cm ($1^1/_4$in) end of piping, so that the cord on the other end will just meet when placed inside. Unpick some of the stitching on the 3cm ($1^1/_4$in) end, trim the piping fabric on the grain so that a small piece can be turned under. Poke the 1cm ($^3/_8$in) size piping end into the other end of the piping and stitch into place. Remove the basting stitches, and set the sachet aside.

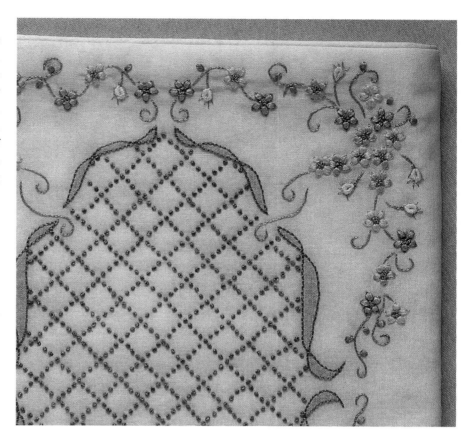

MAKING THE CORD

Cut two 90cm (3ft) lengths of white Perle cotton. Sticky tape one lot of ends to a table. Now twist both the strands tightly, keeping them taut. Twist them in the same direction as the original twist of the strands. Keep twisting until small kinks appear. Place a finger at the centre point of the twisted strands and fold back so that the two ends meet. Remove the cord end from the sticky tape and let the centre go. The cord will twist together. Make a second cord in this manner. Tie knots in the cut ends.

MAKING THE TASSELS

Cut one 3.6m (4yd) length of white Perle cotton. Wind around a 6cm ($2^1/_2$in) wide piece of sturdy cardboard. Cut through all winds on one side. Untwist the end of the cord that was folded back on to itself, opening up a loop. Position the cut tassel lengths into the loop, centring them. Allow the cord to re-twist. Pull the cut

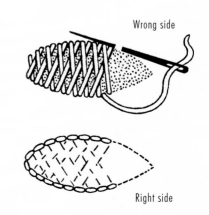

Wrong side

Right side

Shadow Stitch

Diagram 1

Embroider bullions here

Diagram 2

lengths down firmly to form a tassel end. Cut another 60cm (24in) length of Perle cotton and tie one end firmly around the tassel, about 1cm (³/₈in) down from the cord. Wrap this length of cotton around the tassel about ten times, pulling very firmly. Thread a needle with the loose end and end off, pulling the knot under the wrapping.

Cut any excess so it becomes part of the tassel skirt. See Diagrams 1 and 2.

You may wish to finish the tassels by working eight-wrap bullions in two strands of the white embroidery cotton, randomly on the top of the tassel. Then thread a needle with the machine thread and sew the glass beads over and between the bullions.

Trim the tassel ends so that they are neat and straight. A couple of stitches can be placed at the junction of the cords and the tassels, to keep the cord nicely twisted. Make a second tassel in this manner. Pin the knotted ends of both cords to the front of the voile rectangle at the position marked on the pattern, with knots facing outwards. Pin the cords halfway along each short side to keep the knots clear of the machine area.

LINING

For the lining, cut a strip of fabric 44cm x 13cm (17½in x 5in). Machine-stitch a 7mm (¼in) hem across the width of the fabric, on one side only. A second row of stitching can be worked 1mm (¹/₂₅in) from the folded edge.

Cut a second piece of fabric 44cm x 27cm (17½in x 10¾in). Place the machined strip along the bottom edge, right side up.

Fold in half so the piece measures 22cm x 27cm (8¾in x 10¾in). Press on fold line. Machine-stitch the two layers together from A to B along the fold line. See Diagram 3.

Place the embroidered piece, right side down, over the top of the lining. Pin it into place.

Tuck in the tassels and the cord, which was previously pinned into position.

Machine-stitch around sachet over the previous machining, leaving an opening as marked. Trim the seam allowances. Cut knots from the tassel cords. Cut notches at the corners.

Turn to the right side and slip stitch the opening closed.

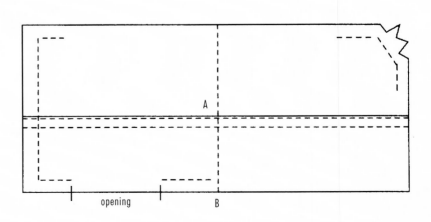

Diagram 3 - Inside pockets
Stitch together along fold line from A to B.

Bullion Rose Set

This elegant coathanger and lingerie bag set would make a perfect gift for someone very special. Cream dupion silk has been used as an elegant background fabric for the embroidery in soft shades of stranded cotton. They are both finished with apricot and cream ribbons.

MATERIALS

- 60cm x 112cm (24in x 44in) cream dupion silk
- DMC Stranded Embroidery Cotton: one skein each of medium flesh (945), very light beige brown (543), green grey (3053), medium yellow beige (3046), ecru
- 2.6m x 3mm (2⁷/₈yd x ¹/₈in) each of double-sided satin ribbon in apricot and cream
- One reel Mettler cotton Art 240 in cream
- 20cm (8in) Lainier iron-on interfacing
- 25cm x 180cm (10in x 71in) quilt batting
- 1m (1¹/₈yd) No 1 cotton piping
- No 9 straw needle
- No 9 crewel needle
- No 26 tapestry needle
- 2.5mm (¹/₈in) twin needle
- No 80 sewing machine needle
- Zipper foot
- Wooden coathanger
- Loop turner (optional)
- Water-erasable pen
- Embroidery hoop (optional)
- Sewing machine
- General Sewing requirements

STITCHES USED

Bullion Stitch, Raised Stem Stitch, Straight Stitch, Ladder Stitch

PREPARATION

COATHANGER

Cut a 45cm (18in) square of silk. Using a water-erasable pen, trace the front and back pattern from the pattern sheet onto the bias grain of the fabric. Mark points A, B, C and D.

If using a hoop, work the embroidery on the uncut piece. Neaten the edges to prevent fraying.

To cover the hook, cut a bias strip 3cm x 30cm (1¹/₄in x 12in). Fold in half lengthwise and machine-sew 7mm (¹/₄in) from fold using a tiny zigzag stitch. Sew for 11cm (4¹/₂in). Use the loop turner to pull through to the right side. Place over hook and use the long bias strip to wrap around the coathanger to secure the hook.

Cut strips of batting 8cm x 180cm (3¹/₈in x 71in). Find the centre of the strip and start wrapping the batting out from the centre of the coathanger, taking care to cover the end well. Sew the end to secure and repeat for the other side.

To make the piping, cut a bias strip 3.5cm x 125cm (1¹/₂in x 49in). If necessary, join the strips on the bias as shown in Diagram 1.

Place the piping cord on the wrong side of the strip and fold over, matching the raw edges together. Using the zipper foot, sew as close to the piping as you can. Gently pull the strip as you sew to make a snug fit.

Trace the design for the bow loops and ribbon onto the pattern piece for the front as shown in the photograph below.

EMBROIDERY

The bow loops and ribbon are worked in raised stem stitch. Using one strand of ecru cotton and the crewel needle, work evenly spaced Straight Stitches 6mm (¹/₄in) apart as shown in Diagram 2. These are the foundation bars. Now using two strands of ecru and a tapestry needle, come up at A and work Raised Stem Stitch

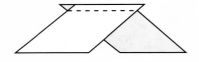

Diagram 1
Joining the bias strip

over and under the foundation bars. Do not take the needle into the fabric until you reach the end of the row. Fasten off on the wrong side of the work. See Diagram 3. The roses and buds, sepals and leaves are all worked in Bullion Stitch.

ROSES

Using two strands of medium flesh (945) cotton in the straw needle, work three 10-wrap bullions close together for the centre of the rose. Change to two strands of very light beige brown (543) and then work three 11-wrap bullions each side of the centre.

ROSEBUDS

With two strands of medium flesh (945), work two 10-wrap bullions for the centre of the bud. With two threads of very light beige brown (543), work one 11-wrap bullion each side of the centre.

SEPALS

Using one strand of green grey (3053) thread, work one 12-wrap bullion each side of roses and buds.

STEMS AND LEAVES

Using a single strand of green grey (3053), work a Straight Stitch for the stems. With the same thread, work two 8-wrap bullions to make a small rounded leaf at the top of the stem. Add other leaves lower down the stem. Finish with two straight stitches in a V-shape at the centre top of the rose.

SMALL FLOWERS

Using two strands of ecru, make small five-petalled flowers by working Straight Stitches three times over into the same holes. To position the petals evenly, imagine a clock face and work one petal at 12 o'clock, one at 2.30, one at 5 o'clock, one at 7.30 and the last at 10 o'clock. Change to one strand of medium yellow beige (3046) and work a three-wrap French Knot in the flower centres.

Using one strand of very light beige brown (543), work double-wrap French Knots at random over the finished embroidery.

ASSEMBLY

Cut out the front and back pieces. Leaving 5cm (2in) of piping free, start at centre front A and use a zipper foot to sew the piping around the outline to B, leaving 5cm (2in) free before cutting off. Clip the seam allowance of the piping around each end.

Sew a line of stay stitching 7mm (¼in) from the bottom of the back piece from C to D. Baste from front to back. Still using the zipper foot, sew from A to C, then from B to D. Leave a gap at A for the hook. Insert the prepared batting-

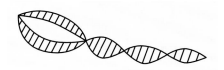

Diagram 2
Work evenly-spaced Straight Stitch bars

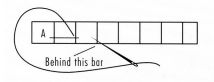

Diagram 3
Work raised stem stitch over straight stitch bars.

Detail of the bullion roses on the coathanger.

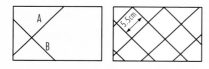

Diagram 4
Grid for pintucking

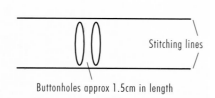

Diagram 5
Stitching buttonholes and casing

measuring bar, only two lines, A and B, need to be marked. Otherwise, mark lines 5.5cm (2⅛in) apart. Using the 2.5mm (⅛in) twin needle, sew line A. Adjust the measuring bar to 5.5cm (2¼in) and sew the next line of pintucks. Continue until all pintucks in this direction have been completed. Then turn the fabric and work the pintucks in the other direction.

EMBROIDERY

In each diagonal square formed by the pintucking, work a rose, leaves and small flowers following the directions given for the coathanger embroidery.

ASSEMBLY

Fold the fabric in half to measure 45cm x 28cm (18in x 11in). Make a French seam down the side of the bag by sewing with the wrong sides together. Trim the seam close to the stitching, and press well. Then, with right sides together, sew a 5mm (¼in) seam. Finish the bottom of the bag in the same manner.

Turn over 6.5cm (2½in) on the top edge of the bag. Mark the positions for two 1.5cm (⅝in) vertical buttonholes on the centre front of the bag, 4.5cm (1¾in) down from the folded top edge. See Diagram 5.

Open out the fold and work the buttonholes. As silk is a very delicate fabric, place a small piece of silk behind the buttonhole positions before you work them.

Refold the top edge and sew either side of the buttonholes to form a casing to take the ribbons. Thread the ribbons through and tie them into a bow.

wrapped coathanger, hook first. Fold under both lower edges and work ladder stitch to close.

Cut one 60cm (24in) length each of cream and apricot ribbon. Tie the ribbons tightly around the hook. Push down to secure and tie into a bow.

PREPARATION

LINGERIE BAG

Cut a piece of dupion silk 45cm x 56cm (18in x 22in). Neaten the edges of the silk to prevent fraying. Using the water-erasable pen, mark the diagonal lines for pintucking. See Diagram 4. If using a

Mountmellick Tablecloth

This style of white-on-white embroidery, worked in soft cotton thread on a closely woven fabric, originated in Ireland.
This cloth is stitched in a variety of textured stitches and the edge is finished with a traditional heavy, knitted fringe.

FINISHED SIZE

- 99cm (39in) square

MATERIALS

- 120cm (47½in) square of Mountmellick cotton jean fabric
- One ball Mountmellick thread
- 10cm (4in) and 15cm (6in) embroidery hoops
- No 22 chenille needles
- Three balls 4-ply white knitting cotton (for fringe)
- 2mm (No 14) knitting needles
- Pencil

STITCHES USED

Buttonhole Stitch, Satin Stitch, Padded Satin Stitch, French Knot, Coral Stitch, Cable Chain, Straight Feather Stitch, Thorn Stitch, Lazy Daisy (Detached Chain) Stitch, Fly Stitch, Saw-tooth Buttonhole Stitch, Cross Stitch, Herringbone Stitch, Whipped Stem Stitch, Fern Stitch, Pistil Stitch, Triple Palestrina Knot Laced Stitch

PREPARATION

Prepare the fabric by washing it in very hot water, using a whitening fabric detergent. Soak for half an hour and then rinse thoroughly in cold water. Flick the excess water away and allow to dry.

The Design Outline (one quarter of the design) on page 45 should be photocopied by 150%, then 200% per cent.

Fold your fabric in half horizontally and vertically and run a line of basting stitches along the folds to mark the fabric into quarters. Trace the design onto all four quarter sections of the fabric, using a light box and pencil or your preferred transfer method (see page 156).

EMBROIDERY

Use the larger embroidery hoop for the floral designs and the small one for the leaf designs.

Embroider the floral and leaf designs with a No 22 chenille needle and a single strand of Mountmellick thread. Refer to the photographs and diagrams.

Stitch illustrations for Thorn Stitch and Triple Palestrina Knot Laced Stitch appear on page 44. All other stitches are shown in the Stitch Guide section, pages 148-151.

SMALL ROSE DESIGN

Rose

Work Buttonhole Stitch (beaded edge outwards) around the petals in the sequence shown in Diagram 1. Add small Straight Stitches in the petals. The sepals are worked in padded satin stitch.

Leaf 1: As a guide, pencil lines at an angle from the centre vein. Fill with a very close Lazy Daisy Stitch. A line of Stem Stitch down the centre forms the vein. See Diagram 2.

Leaf 2: With a pencil, draw the smaller leaf shape inside the main outline. Work Satin Stitch all around the edge of the leaf, then add the centre veins using Fly Stitch,

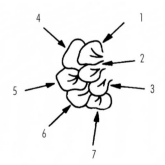

Diagram 1
Small Rose

Diagram 2
Leaf 1

Diagram 3
Leaf 2

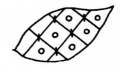

Diagram 4
Leaf 3

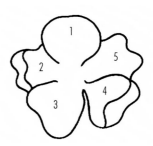

Diagram 5
Large Rose

starting from the tip of the leaf. See Diagram 3.

Leaf 3: Outline the leaf in Thorn stitch, working first one side, then the other, starting at the base. Then lay parallel lines of Straight Stitches one way, then the other way in a trellis pattern. Make a small Straight Stitch over the intersection of each thread and add a single-twist French Knot in each space. See Diagram 4.

Berries

Mass lots of French Knots in the drawn circle. Working four-wrap knots at the centre and three-wrap knots towards the outside, fill the space well.

Stems and branches

All berries, leaves and roses are joined to the main branch with Coral Stitch. Work the main branch from the Thorn Stitch leaf in Cable Chain Stitch.

LARGE ROSE DESIGN

Rose

Buttonhole-stitch all the petal edges in the order given in Diagram 5. Petals No 2 and No 4 have the buttonhole reversed so beading is on the inside edge. Fill the centre with two-wrap French Knots, then add pistil stitch (single twist) stamens.

Refer to Diagram 6 for sequence of working leaves.

Leaf 1: Cable chain down one side of the leaf and come back up on the same side, working a single-wrap French Knot in each chain. Repeat for the other side. Fern stitch the centre vein from the tip to the base.

Leaf 2: Lazy Daisy as before.

Leaf 3: Thorn Stitch and trellis.

Leaf 4: Satin Stitch and feather stitch as before.

Leaf 5: Outline with Stem Stitch, then come back whipping each Stem Stitch

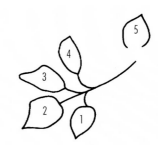

Diagram 6
Leaves (Large Rose)

Diagram 7
Small Leaf Designs

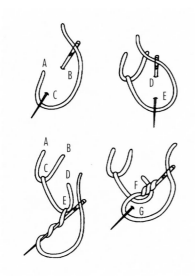

Thorn Stitch

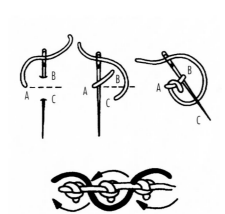

Triple Palestrina Knot Laced Stitch

from the outside in, taking care not to pick up any fabric. Work Herringbone Stitch in the centre, tying down each intersection with a small straight stitch.

Small stems and leaves: The stems are Stem Stitched and the small leaves added in pairs in Lazy Daisy along the stem back to the rose.

Berries: French Knots (four-wrap and three-wrap) as before. Join to the rose with Coral Knot Stitch stems.

Branches: Cable Chain.

SMALL LEAF DESIGN

Refer to Diagram 7 for the sequence of working leaves.

Leaf 1: Outline with Saw-tooth Buttonhole Stitch (alternate three short and three long vertical stitches worked close together). Add three small cross stitches in the centre.

Leaf 2: Cable Chain, French Knots, Fern Stitch centre as before.

Leaf 3: Stem Stitch and Herringbone Stitch as before.

Stems and Branches: Coral Stitch stems join all leaves to Cable Chain main branch.

When all the motifs have been embroidered, work the outside edge

(Scallop Border 1) in Saw-tooth Buttonhole Stitch with the beading on the outside (cutting edge). The longest stitches should be approximately 5mm ($^{1}/_{4}$in). Add a row of Herringbone on the saw-tooth edge, then a row of two-wrap French Knots. The next row (Scallop Border 2) towards the centre is worked in straight Feather Stitch.

Work the final row (Scallop Border 3) in Triple Palestrina Knots, laced first one way and then the other.

FINISHING

Once all the embroidery has been completed, wash the piece well in cold water, then soak to whiten as before. Then iron without starch and cut the edge very close to the buttonhole stitching. You may leave it with this buttonholed edge or add the knitted fringe as directed.

KNITTED FRINGE

Using the three balls of 4-ply white knitting cotton together with the 2mm knitting needles, cast on nine stitches. Every row is the same.

Make one stitch, purl two together, purl one, make one, purl 2 two stitches together, purl one. Continue to the end of the row.

Knit to the required length. Before casting off, attach the edging (overcasting into the buttonhole edge) to ensure the correct length.

Cast off five stitches. Cut the thread and draw through the sixth stitch to finish off. Slip the remaining stitches off the needle and unravel these all along the edge to form the fringe.

MOUNTMELLICK TABLECLOTH

Design Outline

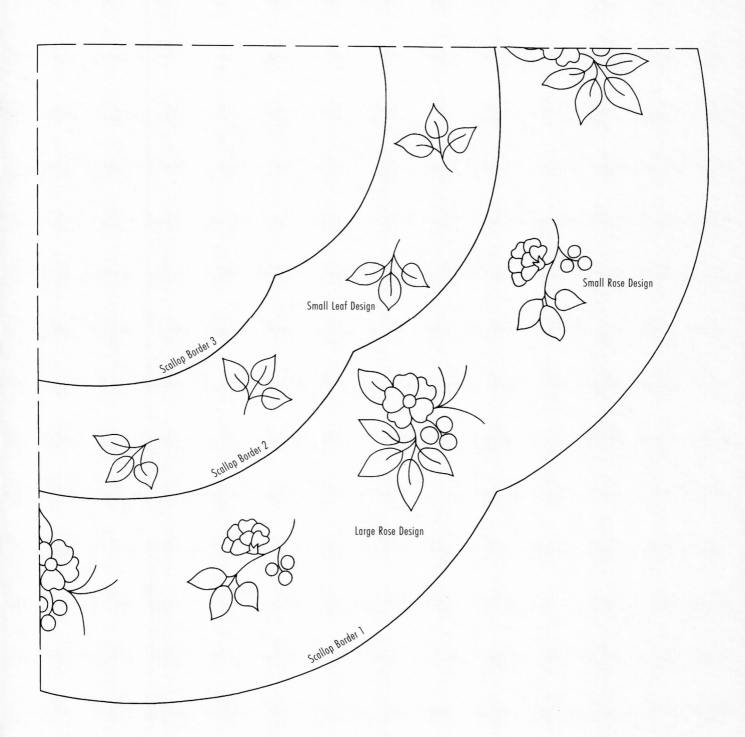

Scallop Border 3

Small Leaf Design

Small Rose Design

Scallop Border 2

Large Rose Design

Scallop Border 1

150%,
then 200%

Pansy Chatelaine

*Sweet purple and red pansies adorn this set of sewing essentials
including a pincushion, scissors case, thimble case and needlebook.
Made in antique gold silk, it is embroidered and trimmed
with Rajmahal Art Silk threads.*

Each pretty pansy face is worked the same way, but by varying the colours you can give each a distinct personality. Use them as shown here on the pincushion, needlebook, scissors case and thimble case, or scatter them on a small tablecloth, blouse pocket, greeting cards, or collars.

PREPARATION

Trace all pattern shapes shown on page 51 onto the silk fabric, allowing a 1cm (³/₈in) wide turning around each. Do not cut out the shapes before completing the embroidery. Use an embroidery hoop and work the appropriate pansy design from the diagrams, following the stitching instructions. When the embroidery is complete, press on the wrong side with your iron on the 'silk' setting.

Cut out each embroidered shape and all the lining shapes (remember to allow a 1cm (³/₈in) turning on each piece). Cut an extra 16cm x 1.5cm (6¹/₂in x ⁵/₈in) piece of silk for the needlebook gusset and a separate piece for the thimble case 11cm x 10cm (4¹/₂in x 4in).

Cut each template shape from card or plastic sheet. Cut batting for the scissors case front and back, needlebook front and back, and thimble case outer shape. Glue the batting to the right side of the appropriate shape.

EMBROIDERY

Refer to the stitch diagrams on page 50 for the stitches and colours used. Directions for specific stitches are in the Stitch Guide on pages 148-151. Two strands of silk thread are used throughout. Some flowers can include an extra row of yellow long and short

stitches between C and D, and E and F. Where there are extra petals shown at the back of some of the larger flowers, add another row of Blanket Stitching in the same colour as F.

CORDS

Each length of cord is made from one skein of pale gold and one skein of deep gold thread. Make six separate lengths of twisted cord using your preferred method.

Put aside two full lengths of cord for the hanging cords.

Whenever the cord is to be cut into lengths for the sewing set items, tightly knot a thread around the cord about 5mm (¹/₄in) either side of the place where you intend to cut. Place a small amount of the craft glue on these ends before cutting and they will not untwist.

LARGE TASSELS

Cut a piece of cardboard 8cm x 6cm (3¹/₄in x 2¹/₂in) and wrap with one skein each of pale gold and deep gold thread. Tie the top of the wraps tightly with six 12cm (5in) strands of thread. Cut through the wraps at the bottom. Hold the cut threads firmly and smooth down starting from the knot at the top. Using a separate length of six threads, tie and knot the bunch of cut threads 1cm (³/₈in) from the top, then wind the remainder of the thread around the knot before ending off with a small oversew stitch. Then trim the tassel evenly at the bottom edge.

Make two tassels and tie them together 1cm (³/₈in) from the top of each tassel. Do not cut off the threads. These will be used later to attach the tassels to the hanging cord.

MATERIALS

- 20cm x 30cm (8in x 12in) antique gold coloured slub silk fabric
- One sheet thin craft card or PVC plasticard (available from railway modelling shops)
- 20cm (8in) fine 0.5mm (¹/₄in) size batting
- 65cm x 2mm (26in x ¹/₁₆in) satin ribbon in antique gold tone
- Small quantity of quilt stuffing for pincushion
- Reel of colour coordinated sewing thread
- Water soluble felt-tipped marking pen
- No 7 straw needle for embroidery
- No 8 crewel needle for stitching the pieces together
- Embroidery scissors
- 15cm embroidery hoop
- Three pieces of fabric 14cm x 6cm (5¹/₂ x 2¹/₂in) for needlebook pages
- Craft glue
- Rajmahal Art Silk: one skein each of violet (115), purple (113), mauve (111), green (805), ecru, black, brown (171), burgundy (379), yellow (94), dark green (65), deep gold (45), dusky pink (243); (for trims) eight skeins each pale gold (44), and deep gold (45)

STITCHES USED

Long and Short Stitch, Satin Stitch, Blanket Stitch, Straight Stitch, Stem Stitch

Detail of the pincushion embroidery.

NEEDLEBOOK

Place the padded front piece face down on to the wrong side of the embroidery. Trim the corners, then glue the turnings over to the back of the card. Cover the padded back and the two lining pieces (cut these fractionally smaller than front and back pieces) in the same way. Fold the gusset piece in half and with a 1cm (³/₈in) seam allowance, stitch across the narrow ends. Turn to the right side. Position the seam in the middle of the gusset and press flat.

Cut the narrow ribbon into two 17.5cm (7in) lengths. Glue the ribbons to the centre front of the wrong sides of each lining section. Glue the gusset to the inner edges of the lining pieces, overlapping them 5mm (¹/₄in) on each side. Glue the padded front and back

pieces on top of the two lining pieces, matching the edges along the gusset.

Stitch through the centre of the three pieces of fabric for the pages. Glue 1cm (³/₈in) at the end of a long hanging cord to the lower edge of the gusset, then glue the stitched spine of the pages down the centre and press to the back of the gusset. Bring the long cord up the centre of these pages and glue in place.

Take another length of cord. Beginning at the centre bottom of the needlebook, leave 4cm (1¹/₂in) of cord free and, with tiny stitches, slip stitch the cord around the outer edges, taking care that you case the corners and gusset curves. Join the two ends of cord at the bottom edge of the gusset by wrapping tightly with sewing thread and ending off with several secure stitches. Cut the cord to match the beginning 4cm (1¹/₂in). Tease out the threads which will form the tassel and if the threads are kinked because of the twisting, simply dampen them to straighten.

PINCUSHION

Cut a piece of backing material to match the embroidered square. Place the wrong sides of the material together and sew around the top and both sides, leaving the bottom edge open. Trim away the excess fabric at the corners and turn to the right side, pulling out the corners to make them square. Stuff the pincushion firmly with quilt stuffing, and turn in the 1cm (⅜in) turning at the bottom before slip-stitching closed.

Cut one length of twisted cord 26cm (10½in) long and two lengths of cord 16cm (6½in) long. Slip stitch the longer cord from the top right-hand corner across the top of the opposite corner, leaving approximately 4cm (1½in) at

each end for the tassels. Once again, leaving 4cm (1½in) at the beginning, stitch one of the shorter pieces of cord from corner to corner across the bottom and leave 4cm (1½in) free at the finish. Repeat with the remaining side. Make the tassels on three corners as before. Finally, stitch the end of the second hanging cord to the top corner of the completed pincushion.

SCISSORS CASE

Cover the front of the scissors case with the embroidered panel. Cover the padded back and two lining pieces with the silk fabric. Glue the lining pieces in position. Leaving 5mm (¼in) open at the top edges, slip stitch the front to the back.

Cut a 9.5cm (4in) length of cord and tuck the ends into the openings and glue into place. Stitch the openings closed and stitch the cord across the top front edge.

Detail of the needlebook embroidery.

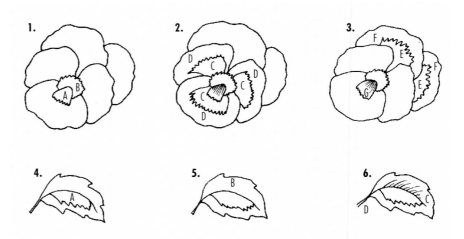

Colour Guide

Diagram 1
A: *Yellow Long and Short Stitch*
B: *Ecru Satin Stitch*

Diagram 2
C: *Black or violet Long and Short Stitch*
D: *Burgundy, purple or mauve Blanket Stitch*
D: *Violet, black or purple Long and Short Stitch*

Diagram 3
E: *Violet, black or purple Long and Short Stitch*
F: *Burgundy, dusky rose or mauve Blanket Stitch*
G: *Brown Straight Stitch shading*

Diagram 4
A: *Light green Satin Stitch*

Diagram 5
B: *Dark green Satin Stitch*

Diagram 6
C: *Gold Stem Stitch leaf vein and Straight Stitch shading*
D: *All stems and stalks in dark green Stem Stitch*

Open a hole at the centre top of the scissors case between the lining and the outer section and glue the other end of the hanging cord which is attached to the pincushion securely in place. Leaving 4cm (1½in) at the centre bottom of the scissors case, stitch the cord up the side, over the top and down the side to the bottom, leaving another 4cm (1½in) of cord loose. Make a tassel as before.

THIMBLE CASE

Leaving 5mm (¼in) open at the top and bottom of the thimble case padded outer shape, top sew the back seam. Sew two lengths of cord around the top and bottom edges, tucking the ends into the openings and then stitching them closed. Cover and fit the base piece. Top-stitch in place.

Sew the back seam of the lining and trim the seam to 5mm (¼in). Glue both sides of the seam to one side of the stitching line and turn right side out. Make a tiny hem around the top edge. Run a row of gathering stitches around the bottom edge, pulling it in slightly before ending off securely with several tiny oversew stitches.

Cover the base lining piece and run craft glue around the inside gathered edge of the lining. Push this base down the tube of hemmed fabric, right side uppermost, so that it sits firmly against the gathered edge. Glue the wrong side of the base lining and gathered edges and press into position inside the thimble case. Spread a little glue around the inside of the thimble case and secure the lining to the card-covered shape. Glue the other end of the hanging cord which is attached to the needlebook to the inside of the thimble case. Sew the remaining 30cm (12in) length of satin ribbon to the back seam of the lining, about 1cm (⅜in) from the top edge, and tie in a bow gathering the top of the bag closed.

FINISHING

Arrange the two hanging cords over a door handle or hook so that the needlebook hangs lowest, then the scissors case, pincushion and finally thimble case. Thread a needle with six strands of silk thread and sew the two tassels to the loop, then wind the remaining thread around the cord several times to finish off. Stitch to secure.

PANSY CHATELAINE
Design and Embroidery Outlines

Scissors Case

Cut here for front

Thimble Case

Thimble Case Base

Thimble Case Base Lining

Pincushion

Needle Case

115%

Fabulous Frame-ups

You'll want to frame these stunning designs. What's more, single motifs or letters from the samplers included in this section can be adapted to decorate and personalise tray mats, napkins, bookmarks, blouse pockets or anything else you can think of.

Fairy Wrens in my Garden

*The personality of these well-loved Australian birds is captured
in this embroidery. Their bodies are built up in felt before being embroidered,
to give a realistic appearance. The branches and blossoms are worked
in a combination of surface stitchery and stumpwork.*

NEEDLELACE PAD

There are various ways to make a pad for working the needlelace petals: Two small 8cm (3in) squares of light-coloured felt glued together lightly with fabric glue applied to a thin line around the edge only. Or, a rectangle of heavy cotton fabric folded into three. Or, two squares or circles of calico with a piece of Pellon between, stitched together around the edge. Whichever method you choose, the pad should be covered on one side with a piece of clear adhesive film.

PREPARATION

Wrap the inner rings of your embroidery hoop with light-coloured bias binding. This provides greater grip and keeps the fabric taut. Using a lightbox or window and a fine HB pencil, trace the surface embroidery design on page 58 onto the right side of the background fabric. Mount this and the larger square of calico together in the larger hoop and pull both layers taut before tightening the screw very firmly. Always work with clean hands, avoiding the use of hand cream before embroidering, because stumpwork cannot be washed, care needs to be taken.

SURFACE EMBROIDERY

One strand of thread is used throughout, unless otherwise specified.

BRANCH

Using a single strand of 640 thread, work the stems in Stem Stitch. Work them with one or two extra rows of Stem Stitch towards the right-hand side to thicken the stem slightly.

LEAVES

Starting with the leaves towards the ends of the stems, work a line of Back Stitch around the outline of the leaf with 3024. Using the same colour, work slanting Satin Stitch from the leaf tip to about half-way down the leaf. Work from the centre vein to the outside, making sure you keep the stitch slanting and covering the Back Stitch, which is there only to give a firm edge to work over. Fill in the rest of the leaf with 3033. Use a combination of greens – 3024, 3052, 3053 – to work all the leaves on the background fabric. Note that the leaves at the extremities of the branches are lighter than those towards the centre of the picture which are darker.

WRENS

Refer to Diagram 1. Working the female (standing on the ground) first, stitch the tail with long Straight Stitches from the

FINISHED SIZE

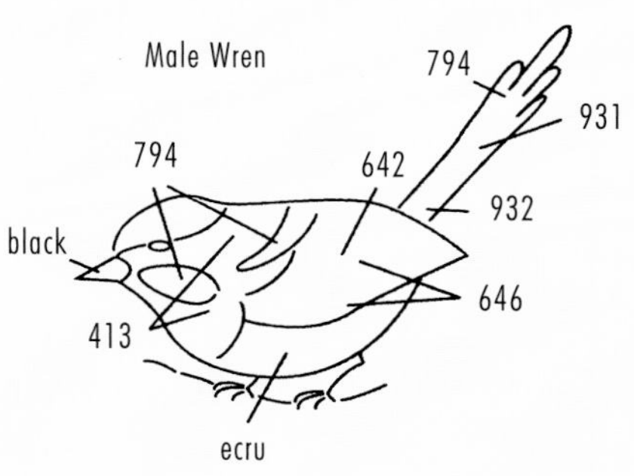

• 18cm x 10cm (7in x 4in)

MATERIALS

• 36cm (14in) square background fabric

• 36cm (14in) square calico or homespun

• 15cm (6in) square calico or homespun

• Pellon (optional)

• DMC Stranded Embroidery Cotton: one skein each of very dark beige grey (640), very light brown grey (3024), medium green grey (3052), green grey (3053), ecru, black, dark pewter grey (413), dark beige grey (642), medium beige grey (644), dark beaver grey (646), light cornflower blue (794), dark antique blue (930), medium antique blue (931), peach flesh (353)

• Minnamurra Hand-dyed Stranded Cotton: one skein of peach/pink variegated (50)

• 35cm (14in) length of 30 gauge cake wire: two in green, seven in white

• No 8 or 9 crewel needle

• Large darner or chenille needle

• 10cm (4in) square piece of light grey or light brown felt

• Two small black beads for eyes

• Small, sharp embroidery scissors

• Needlelace working pad (see note above)

• 25cm (10in) embroidery hoop

• 10cm (4in) embroidery hoop

• Embroidery magnifier (optional)

• Fine HB pencil

• The example shown uses low-sheen Empress Satin furnishing fabric but any firm, smooth, closely woven fabric in your preferred colour should be suitable.

STITCHES USED

Stem Stitch, Satin Stitch, Back Stitch, Straight Stitch, Buttonhole Stitch, Fly Stitch, Corded Brussels Stitch, Ladder Stitch, Lazy Daisy (Detached Chain) Stitch, Cast-On Stitch

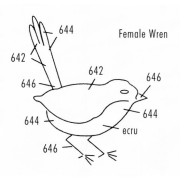

Diagram 1

Diagram 2

base of tail to the tip. Use 644 towards the front and 642 towards the back, adding one or two stitches in 646 for shading.

Refer to the wren templates on the Pattern Sheet. From the felt, cut out one of each body piece for the female wren. Lay the smallest piece of felt (a) in the centre of the outlined body and catch through the background fabric with a stab stitch at each end using one strand of 642. Piece (b) is placed over the first and attached in the same way, then piece (c), which will need a stitch on each side as well as at each end. The largest body piece (d) is placed over the three previous pieces, but this time bring the needle up through the background fabric on the pattern line and down through the edge of the felt, keeping the stitches about 5mm ($\frac{1}{4}$in) apart around the edge and allowing the felt to mound slightly over the previous layers.

Using ecru thread and long, slanting Straight Stitches, work the wren's breast from the hue of the wing over the edge of the felt. Work a few short stitches in 644 on the throat, with some more stitches in the same colour among the ecru stitches towards the rear of the underbelly, for a little shading. With 642 carefully work over the top of the head, back and wing in long and short stitches, remembering the natural direction of the feathers.

NOTE: Once you have worked the head, the stitches down the rest of the bird should be quite long to achieve the appearance of feathers. A few stitches running in the same direction in 646 will help this, with a line of 646 at the edge of the wing.

A few Straight Stitches in 646 form the beak. Attach the bead for the eye at this stage, to bring the bird to life. Using one strand of black thread, mount a small black bead where indicated, with the hole uppermost, and attach with three stitches to hold in place. Work the legs and feet

with Straight Stitches in 646. Work the tail for the male wren as you did for the female, rising 794 at the front, 931 and 930 for the shading. Cut out and attach the felt for the male in the same way as for the female. Using 794 and long and short straight stitches, work the top of the head. Continue working the bands of colour as shown in Diagram 2, merging the colours at the edge of the bands to avoid a hard line where the colours join. Add the beak in black and the eye as before. Work the feet to curl over the branch in straight stitch using 646.

DETACHED EMBROIDERY

DETACHED LEAVES

Mount the smaller square of calico tightly into the smaller hoop. Cut each length of green wire into three pieces. Bend one piece of wire in half, pinching it to make a pointed tip and shaping the wire as shown in Diagram 3 on page 58. Do not cut off the ends of the wire, as these are used to attach the leaf when assembling the piece. Using one strand of 3052, catch the wire to the calico in three or four places, with a stitch to hold the two wires together at the base.

Still using 3052, work close Buttonhole stitch over the wire around the outside of the leaf (loops on the outside of the wire),

Stitching the leaves.

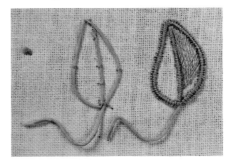

working through the calico and keeping the stitches very close up against the wire.

Fill the leaf with a series of close Fly Stitches, keeping the stitches slanting as you did on the background fabric and allowing no calico to show through the stitching. The detached leaves should also have some variation in colour as for the surface stitchery leaves. Work five leaves.

When all the leaves have been worked, cut out as closely as possible to the outside of the Buttonhole Stitches, holding your scissors on a slant and taking care not to cut the stitching. Carefully trim off any 'whiskers'. Store all these leaves safely, as it is very easy to misplace them.

Corded Brussels Stitch.

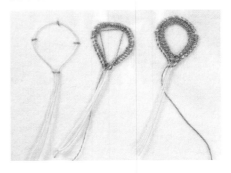

NEEDLELACE PETALS

Cut all lengths of white wire into four pieces. Shape one piece of wire to the pattern shape shown in Diagram 4. With a strand of the variegated Minnamurra thread, attach the wire to the adhesive film-covered side of the needlelace pad with one stitch to the top, one stitch to each side and one at the base of the petal to hold the two wires together. Again, do not cut off the extending wires. Finish off by taking a couple of stitches into the back of the felt pad.

Tie one end of the variegated thread to the wire at the base of the petal, leaving about 5cm (2in) hanging. Work Buttonhole Stitch over the wire, this time with the Buttonhole loops on the inside of the wire, and stitching only over the wire, not through the felt pad. Leave about a needle width between the stitches.

The stitches should be firm but not tight. When you have stitched right around the petal, again tie the thread to the wire at the base, then carry the thread to the top of the petal, pick up the loop of one of the Buttonhole Stitches at the top right-hand corner, cross to the top left-hand corner and pick up another loop then go down to the base of the petal where you will again pick up a loop. (If you are left-handed, these directions may be reversed.) Work another row of Buttonhole Stitches, picking up the loop of the buttonhole in the previous row and the carried thread (corded brussels stitch). Repeat this for each row; you will need fewer stitches in each row as you work towards the centre. Continue in this manner until the petal is filled. If you find you have a small gap in the middle of the petal this can be closed with two or three Ladder Stitches. Tie the thread ends together and leave them hanging. When the filling is complete, cut the holding threads at the back of the pad and lift the petal gently. Work one petal at a time and cut off before going on to the next one. Again, store these little petals carefully until needed. You will need 28 of these petals, but they are quite quick to do.

FOREGROUND

Work horizontal Straight Stitches in varying lengths using 640 and 3053 with some more stitches in 640 to represent twigs on the ground. Some tufts of grass may be added by working Straight Stitches in 3052.

ASSEMBLY

Decide where you want to place the detached leaves. Insert the large chenille needle up to the eye straight through the

background fabric at this spot to open the fabric sufficiently. Slide both wires of the leaf together down alongside the eye.

Pull through from the back until the base of the leaf is resting against the fabric. Turn the hoop over, bend the wires in opposite directions at the back of the work and attach for about 2cm (1in) by working a few overcast stitches into the backing calico only. It is a good idea to attach the wire along the line of a stem or the back of a leaf or flower if possible, so the wires will not show through when the piece is mounted. When you have attached the wire for this distance, bend it back on itself and hold with a few more stitches before cutting off the surplus wire. Attach the other leaves in the same way and bend gently to the desired shape.

Attach the petals into the positions indicated, five petals to each full flower, threading the two wires from each to the wrong side around the centre of the flower in the same way as for the leaves. Take the hanging threads through to the back at the same time.

Turn your work over, take one wire from two adjacent petals and catch down as before. By taking one wire from each of two petals the attachment will be more stable and secure. Attach all the petals in this way, noting that the buds are made with only one petal which is bent slightly in on itself. The side-view flowers have two or three petals, with sepals worked in Lazy Daisy Stitch in 3052, taking care to keep the stitches narrow, but not tight, so that the petals will stand away from the background. Work a calyx and short stem in the same colour to join to the branch. Do the same for the buds.

The centres of the flowers are worked with two strands of 353. Spiral several 10-wrap cast-on stitches around the centre, overlapping the stitches as you would for a bullion rose. The outer of these stitches will be worked through the needlelace petals to form a thick, frilly centre to the flowers. Gently bend the petals to a pleasing shape. Add your initials and date if desired. Remove from the hoop and press carefully to remove hoop marks. Do not press the entire piece.

FAIRY WRENS IN MY GARDEN
Surface Embroidery Design

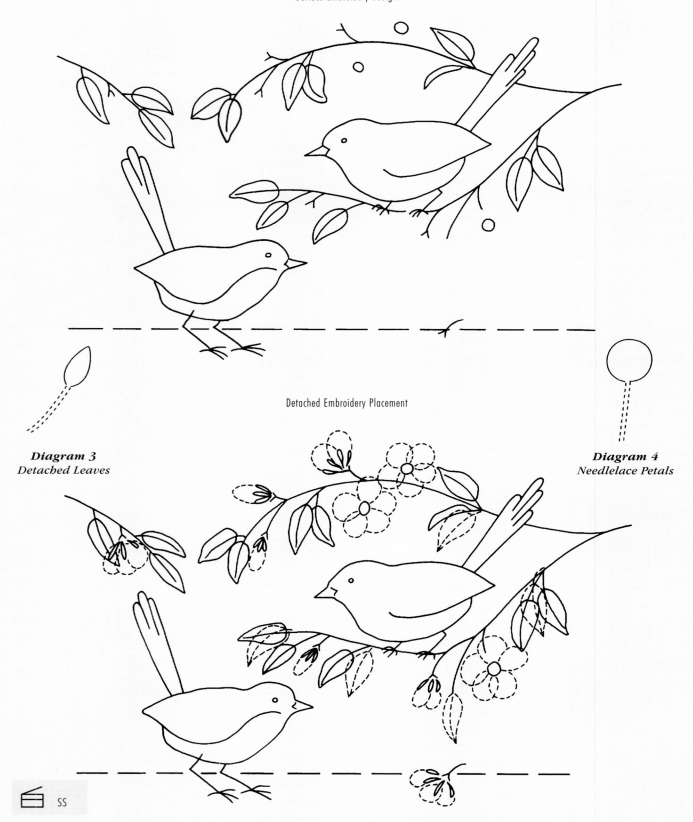

Detached Embroidery Placement

Diagram 3
Detached Leaves

Diagram 4
Needlelace Petals

SS

Pansy Garland

Delicate pinks, mauve and yellow give this garland a gentle,
old-world feeling. It is worked mainly in long and short satin stitch
using a single thread of stranded cotton. To add an aged look,
the finished embroidery has been dyed in coffee.

FINISHED SIZE

• 10cm (4in) diameter

MATERIALS

• 30cm (12in) square closely woven cotton fabric such as homespun

• DMC Stranded Embroidery Cotton:
one skein each of light pink (225),
medium green (523), lemon (677),
blue (932), light mauve (3042),
dark plum pink (3726), black (310),
light gold (676), dark gold (781),
dark mauve (3041), dark green (3363),
medium dusty pink (3727)

• No 10 crewel needle

• No 10 straw needle

• Embroidery hoop (optional)

• Tracing paper

• Fineline marker pen

• Water-soluble pen or pencil

STITCHES USED

Long and Short Satin Stitch, French Knots,

Lazy Daisy (Detached Chain) Stitch, Back Stitch,

Buttonhole Stitch, Straight Stitch

PREPARATION

Trace the design outline from page 61. Find the centre of the fabric and transfer the design to your fabric using a lightbox and water-soluble pen or using your preferred method.

EMBROIDERY

The embroidery is worked throughout using one strand of cotton. Refer to the Shading Guide colours to use and the direction of the stitches. The denser shading on the diagram represents the darker colours on the pansies, the more spaced shading represents the black pansy 'face'. A crewel needle is used for all embroidery except French Knots, which are worked with a straw needle.

Pansies

Following the shading diagram on the opposite page, embroider the shading on the back and side petals of the pansies in Long and Short Satin Stitch. Embroider the outer edge of these petals with the lighter colour. Overlap the stitches to blend the colours and ensure there is no ridge. Using the colour specified, stitch the entire bottom petals. Using dark gold thread (781), embroider the centre of the pansies in Buttonhole Stitch.

Using dark green (3363), work a Lazy Daisy Stitch each side of the centre. With straw needle and dark plum pink thread (3726), add a single-wrap French Knot at the top of the centre.

Finally, embroider the 'face' of the pansy with Straight Stitches, graduating them as shown in the photograph.

Pansy Buds

Working in Long and Short Satin Stitch, use the darker of the specified shades to work the under-petal first, then stitch the top petal in the lighter shade. Embroider two Lazy Daisy Stitches in dark green (3363) at the base of the bud. Work the stem in dark green (3363) using tiny back stitches.

Leaves

Using dark green, embroider the top of the leaves in Long and Short Satin Stitch. Change to light green and embroider the bottom of the leaf, overlapping the stitches to blend the cotton and avoid making a ridge.

Forget-me-nots

These are optional and are not marked on the design outline. Refer to the photograph for placement. Using the straw needle, embroider five single-wrap French Knots in a close circle. Add a single-wrap French Knot in dark gold (781) at the centre of each flower. Do not pass the thread between flowers as it may show through to the front of the work and spoil the finished effect.

DYEING

To give a mellow, aged effect, you may wish to dye the piece. First rinse the completed embroidery. In a large bowl, mix four cups of boiling water and four teaspoons of instant coffee. Stir the mixture well to dissolve.

Soak the fabric for approximately fifteen minutes and then soak again in clean, lukewarm water for five minutes.

Change the water and soak with one teaspoon of white vinegar diluted in the water (this restores the lustre to the thread). Do not wring. Place face down on a light-coloured, fluffy towel and press on the wrong side until dry. Your finished piece may be framed or made up into a cushion with a ruffle in a small floral print in similar colours.

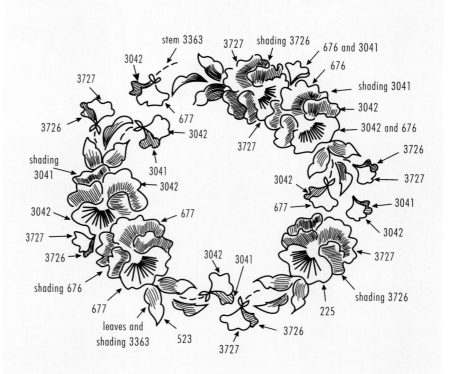

SHADING GUIDE AND STITCH DIRECTION

DESIGN OUTLINE

115%

Antique Alphabet Sampler

In centuries past, a young girl learnt her alphabet
as she stitched her sampler. This pretty floral design, worked in
cross stitch using stranded cotton, is reminiscent
of those early examples.

FINISHED SIZE

• 50cm x 32cm (20in x 13in) (design only)

MATERIALS

• 60cm x 70cm (24in x 28in) 25-count cream evenweave linen

• Anchor Stranded Cotton: one skein each of gold (305), powder blue (976), sky blue (977), deep sky blue (978), teal (979), light pink (968), dusty rose (969), pink mauve (970), sage (208), jade (216), deep emerald (217), light dusty pink (893), dusty pink (894), deep dusty pink (895), claret (896), dusty blue mauve (939), blue mauve (176), deep blue mauve (177), light aqua (160), aqua (161), deep aqua (162), sea foam (265), olive (266), avocado (268), coral (1022), blush (1023), deep blush (1024), henna (1025), light grey/green (859), grey/green (860), deep grey/green (861), light dusty mauve (870), dusty mauve (871), deep dusty mauve (872); two skeins of tan (309); five skeins of old gold (306)

• No 24 tapestry needle

STITCHES USED

Cross Stitch

PREPARATION

Before you begin, overlock the raw edges to prevent fraying. Find the fabric centre by measuring or folding the fabric in quarters. Sew a loose running stitch along the folds to mark the centre. Where the lines cross in the centre of the fabric corresponds with the centre of the design. The Design Chart on the Pattern Sheet has an arrow on each side, so using a ruler, draw a light line to join arrows which gives you the design centre. You can either start stitching at the centre and work outwards, or use the centre mark to count up to where you wish to begin. Each square on the Design Chart represents a cross stitch and each symbol represents the colour to use. Work the stitches over two threads at a time using three strands of cotton throughout.

STITCHING

You may stitch from left to right or right to left, whichever is most comfortable for you. However, all the top stitches must travel in the same direction throughout the embroidery.

To begin stitching, select your thread, separate three threads and allow them to unwind. Put the threads back together and thread into your needle. Bring the needle from the back of the fabric at the point where you wish to begin stitching. Hold a length of the cotton at the back and work the first stitches over this thread, securing it.

To end off your thread, run the needle and thread through the back of several stitches.

Try to keep your tension even. An embroidery hoop will make it easier to keep an even tension and will give better results. Do not carry thread across the back from letter to letter as the thread might show through to the front when the embroidery is finished.

If work becomes soiled, wash in hot water with mild soap. Rinse well and dry flat. Do not wring. To press, place a light-coloured fluffy towel on an ironing board and lay the embroidery face down. Press with a warm iron.

Your work is completed and is now ready to be framed.

Heritage Cross Stitch

These designs were inspired by an ornate cast-iron balustrade pattern that was popular in Adelaide in Victorian times and a traditional appliqué quilt pattern of the Mennonite people in Canada. Mount your creations to decorate a tray.

CANADIAN QUILT

FINISHED SIZE

- 16.5cm square (6¹/₂in)

MATERIALS

- 30cm (12in) square 30-count white linen (14-count white Aida can be substituted — the design will be a little larger but will still fit the tray)
- DMC Stranded Embroidery Cotton: one skein each of deep pink (3688), light pink (3689), yellow (676), green (524), and blue-green (927)
- 24cm (9¹/₂in)square Sudberry House display tray
- No 26 tapestry needle
- General sewing requirements

STITCHES USED

Cross Stitch, Back Stitch

PREPARATION

Many cross stitch projects give instructions to begin stitching in the centre of the design. An alternative is to begin at the top left of the piece and watch the design as it develops from the top down.

To begin like this, find the centre of the fabric by folding it in half horizontally and then vertically. With a needle threaded with one strand of cotton, come up in the centre and run a line of basting stitches to the top of the fabric, making sure that each basting stitch is exactly the length of five cross stitches (five spaces on Aida or ten threads on linen. Now count up this row until you have reached the height of the first stitch (33 stitches up for Iron Lace, 56 stitches up for Quilt). This is easy to do because you can count up in blocks of five cross stitches for each basting stitch.

With your needle again threaded with a single strand, bring the needle up at this point on the centre line and run another row of basting stitches out to the left side of the fabric, again making sure that each basting stitch covers the space of five cross stitches. Now count across this line the number of spaces you require (46 stitches for Iron Lace, 50 stitches for Quilt).

This is where you start stitching.

STITCHING

Enlarge the graphs on pages 68-69 so they are easy to follow. Both designs are stitched using two strands of thread over two threads of linen. Work the cross stitch in horizontal rows, from left to right for the first half of each stitch and returning from right to left to complete the stitches. Left-handed stitchers may wish to work the opposite way. Work the back stitch in dark green thread using two strands for extra definition.

FINISHING

After all the stitching is finished, it is a good idea to wash the piece. This not only removes any dirt or skin oils the fabric may have picked up, but also refreshes the natural sizing found in cotton or linen, giving it a smoother appearance. Launder in lukewarm water with a small amount of mild soap. Do not leave the piece to soak, but swish it through the water. Rinse very well in warm then cool water and wrap in a towel to absorb moisture.

Gently iron dry with the stitching face down on a fluffy light-coloured towel. It is now ready for framing or finishing.

ADELAIDE IRON LACE

FINISHED SIZE

- 12cm x 17.5cm (5in x 7in)

MATERIALS

- 30cm x 35cm (12in x 14in) 28-count Permin linen in teal (40)
- DMC Stranded Embroidery Cotton: one skein each of white, light green (927), medium green (926) and dark green (924)
- No 24 tapestry needle
- Tray to fit (optional)
- General sewing requirements

STITCHES USED

Cross Stitch, Back Stitch

CANADIAN QUILT

Graph

DMC Stranded Cotton

| | 3688 | | 3689 | | 676 | | 524 | | 927 |

ADELAIDE IRON LACE
Graph

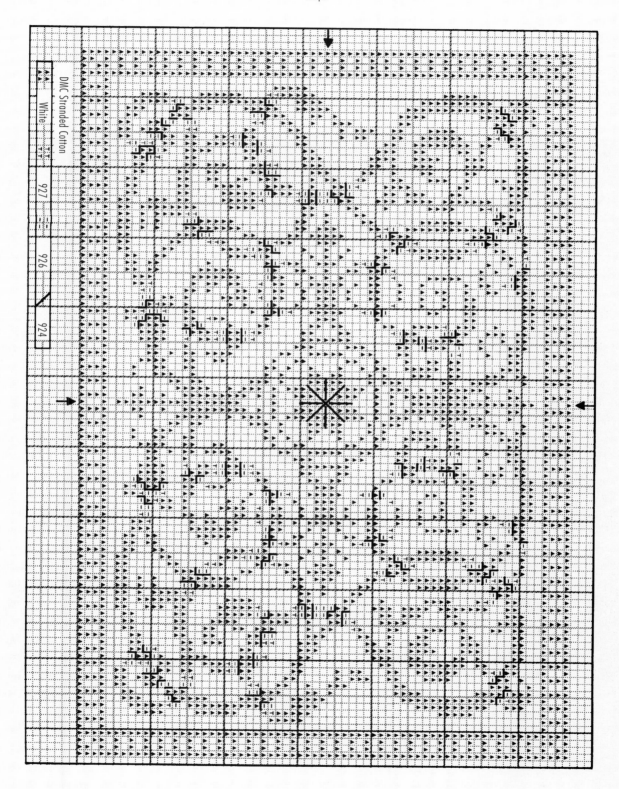

The Prettiest Frame-up

*The fresh white and soft floral shades of this photo mat of
perforated paper are embroidered with silk ribbon and stranded
cotton. The perfect finish for a cherished image,
this delicate design is created using only basic stitches.*

EMBROIDERING THE DESIGN

Use three strands of white cotton to embroider the frame and grid pattern, following the Stitching Guide on page 72. Only the bottom half of the pattern is given on the Pattern Sheet, the top half being a mirror image. Each line on the graph represents one grid of perforated paper.

Stitch the outer border in cross stitch, then work the four corner motifs before counting inwards from the centre of each side to establish the position of the oval. Cross stitch the oval outline. Then, using six strands of thread, Satin Stitch hearts in the corners. Back-stitch all diagonal lines using three strands of cotton.

Work all the lines in one direction before turning the work and stitching the opposite way. Finally, embroider the straight stitch groups in the scallops of the outer edges. Work the ribbon flowers following the Stitching Guide. Use short lengths of ribbon, working one group of flowers at a time, to avoid carrying lengths of ribbon across the back of the work. The design is shown in one corner of the Graph only as a guide. Start with the large rose, centring it over the grid lines which cross the middle of the corner. Establish the outer points of the spray by stitching the lavender at each end, then fill in the rest of the flowers and leaves between these points. Working on each of the four motifs in turn will help to keep them looking the same. Extra flowers, buds or leaves can be added if necessary to fill in any gaps.

CUTTING AND MOUNTING

After completing the embroidery, cut out the centre oval. Using a sharp craft knife,

make a cut along the next line of holes beyond the stitching on one of the long sides of the oval. With sharp pointed scissors, carefully work around the oval, trimming away the centre piece and leaving a margin of one grid of paper.

Trim the outer edge of the design in the same way as before, maintaining a margin of one grid of paper.

Mount the photograph using double-sided sticky tape in each corner, taking care to place it centrally on the rectangle of mat board. Apply small pieces of tape to the back of the embroidery behind the corner hearts and the centres of the long sides, then carefully position the embroidery panel over the photograph you wish to frame and press firmly in place. The assembled piece is now ready for framing.

If you wish to use glass, professional framing is suggested for an elegant finishing touch.

MATERIALS

- 35cm x 22.5cm (14in x 9in) white perforated paper
- DMC Stranded Embroidery Cotton: two skeins of white
- 3mm (1/8in) wide silk embroidery ribbon: 2.5m (30in) each of pale pink, dark pink, pale blue-green, grass green, dark grass green, lavender, pale golden yellow and dark blue
- 26cm x 21cm (10½in x 8½in) matt board
- Double-sided sticky tape
- General sewing requirements
- Sharp craft knife

STITCHES USED

Cross Stitch, Satin Stitch, Back Stitch, Straight Stitch, Fern Stitch, French Knots, Lazy Daisy (Detached Chain) Stitch, Fly Stitch

THE PRETTIEST FRAME-UP
Stitching Guide

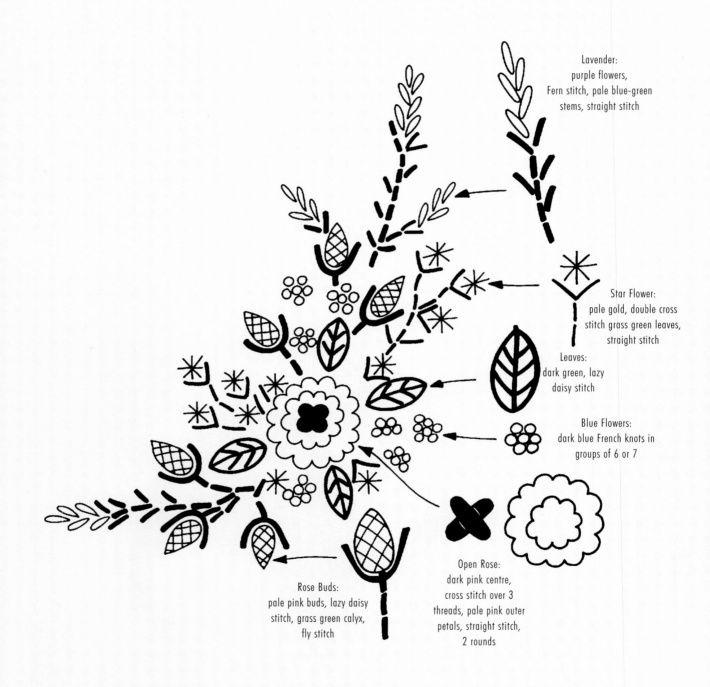

Lavender:
purple flowers,
Fern stitch, pale blue-green
stems, straight stitch

Star Flower:
pale gold, double cross
stitch grass green leaves,
straight stitch

Leaves:
dark green, lazy
daisy stitch

Blue Flowers:
dark blue French knots in
groups of 6 or 7

Rose Buds:
pale pink buds, lazy daisy
stitch, grass green calyx,
fly stitch

Open Rose:
dark pink centre,
cross stitch over 3
threads, pale pink outer
petals, straight stitch,
2 rounds

Spanish Intrigue

*There's an air of romance and mystery about this design created
using stranded cotton, cross stitch and back stitch.
If only you could peep behind the ornately decorated wrought-iron door into
the courtyard beyond, what story might unfold?*

FINISHED SIZE

• 10cm (4in) square (design only)

MATERIALS

• 30cm (12in) square 14-count white Aida cloth

• Anchor Stranded Cotton: one skein each of olive (844), peach cream (1010), peach (336), rust (1004), mushroom (898), light grey (399), deep grey (235), charcoal (1041), white (1), black (403), dusty peach (10), blush (11), light sage (214), sage (215), deep sage (216), light dusty green (264), avocado (266), deep avocado (269),
deep peach (337), cream beige (830)

• No 24 tapestry needle

• Embroidery hoop (optional)

• Pencil

• Frame to fit (optional)

STITCHES USED

Cross Stitch, Back Stitch

PREPARATION

❖

Before commencing the embroidery, overlock the raw edges of the fabric to prevent it from fraying.

Fold the fabric in halves, horizontally and vertically, to find the centre. Sew a line of running stitches along each fold. The point where the stitches intersect is the centre of the fabric.

After photocopying and enlarging the graph on page 75, draw a light line from the top to the bottom arrow and from the left to the right arrow.

The lines will intersect at the centre of the design (corresponding with the lines stitched on the fabric). Each square on the design graph opposite represents a cross stitch, and each symbol represents the colour to use.

STITCHING

❖

The design is worked throughout in three strands for cross stitch and one strand for back stitch. Work all cross stitch first, then back stitch according to instructions.

To begin stitching, separate three threads and allow them to untwist completely before rejoining and threading into the needle. Bring the needle through the fabric, leaving a loose end at the back. Hold that end of the thread against the fabric and secure it with the first few cross stitches. To end off the thread, simply weave the needle through the back of several stitches to secure it. Try to keep your tension even. An embroidery hoop or frame will make it easier and give you better results.

When all the cross stitch has been

complete, work the back stitch. The branches of the tree are worked in mushroom (898), the lines on the path in light grey (399), and the decorative detail on the door and window in black (403).

FINISHING

❖

Before framing, it is a good idea to wash the work to remove any dirt or skin oils that may have accumulated. Wash in hot water with mild soap. Swish the fabric through the water, but do not squeeze it. Rinse well. Do not wring, and dry flat. Place face down on a light-coloured, fluffy towel and press on the wrong side so as not to flatten the stitching. Professional framing will enhance your work.

SPANISH INTRIGUE

Graph

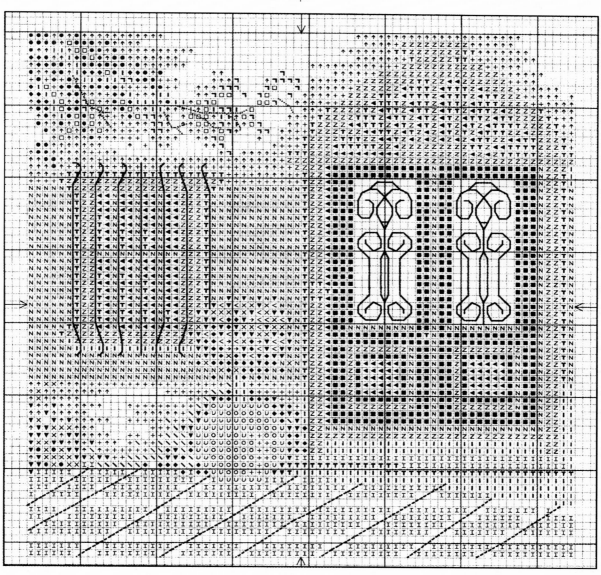

COLOUR KEY

Anchor Stranded Cotton

⧄⧄ 844	≪≪ 10
↑↑ 1010	⇥⇥ 11
++ 336	⌐⌐ 214
∪∪ 1004	□□ 215
⌷⌷ 898	●● 216
NN 399	×× 264
TT 235	▼▼ 266
◀◀ 1041	●● 269
ZZ 1	○○ 337
■■ 403	II 830

Pretty and Practical

Turn an afternoon cuppa into an elegant event with an embroidered tea-cosy and delightful old-fashioned placemats, or pamper yourself with a needlework set that will capture the heart of any cat lover. The projects in this section all have practical applications, and will give you pleasure every time you use them.

Wool Embroidered Tea-cosy

This very stylish tea-cosy is embroidered with pink three-dimensional roses and buds and worked in wool in cast-on stitch. Mohair, silk ribbon and shiny rayon thread add interesting textures and highlights.

PREPARATION

Photocopy the Design Outline on page 82 at 160%. Fold the blanketing in half and position the pattern on the fold. Mark the position of the roses. It is not necessary to transfer the entire design.

NOTE: If using a hoop, do not cut out the tea-cosy pattern until all embroidery has been completed.

If you prefer to work on a smaller piece of blanketing, cut out the shape but it will not be possible to use a hoop.

STEP 1: Using darkest colour, work first petal with 12 cast-ons, second petal 15 cast-ons, third petal 18 cast-ons.

EMBROIDERY

The roses are worked in Cast-on Stitch using one strand of wool and the No 1 milliners' needle. See Diagram 1 below for the method of working the stitch and Diagram 2 for the sequence of working the petals.

The roses are worked in three colours for the smaller size and four colours for the larger size. Vary your choice of colour combinations, but always start with the darkest of your chosen colours and work out to the lightest. Pull each petal tight to give a frilled effect.

For example, work the first three petals in 900, the next round of five petals in 902, and the third round of eight petals in 903. For a larger rose, add a fourth round of petals in 905. Start some roses with 902 and work out to 964. Once all the roses are stitched, add the Fly-

Diagram 1
Stitching the Roses

FINISHED SIZE

- 30cm x 25cm (12in x 10in)

MATERIALS

- 26cm x 32cm (10½in x 12½in) cream wool blanketing (or desired size to fit your teapot)
- Sufficient batting to line the blanketing with double thickness
- Fabric for lining
- Paterna Wool Persian Yarn: one skein each of rose pinks (900), (902), (903), (905), (964); greens (D556), (D546), (600), (602)
- Little Wood Fleece 3-ply Gossamer Mohair: one skein of cornflower blue
- 2m x 4mm (2yd x ¼in) YLI silk ribbon in gold (54)
- Edmar Glory Thread: one skein of light forest green (167)
- 2m x 24mm (2yd x 1in) double-sided satin ribbon in two shades of rose pink
- 60cm (24in) narrow piping cord
- No 20 and 22 chenille needles
- No 1 milliners' needle
- Water-soluble fabric pen
- Embroidery hoop (optional)
- Needle threader for milliners' needle

STITCHES USED

Cast-On Stitch, Straight Stitch,

Lazy Daisy (Detached Chain) Stitch,

Fly Stitch, Couching, French Knot

STEP 2: Change to lighter colour and work first petal with 20 cast-ons. The next petal starts halfway around the first with 22 cast-ons. Continue in this manner with 24 cast-ons, then 25 cast-ons and finally 26 cast-ons.

STEP 3: Change to lighter colour. Work eight petals as before, each with 28 cast-ons. If a fourth round is required, only work the petals three quarters of the way around the rose tapering from the side of the rose, around the bottom up to the other side. This will give the rose a fuller bottom. Start the side petal half way around the last petal of the previous row, working 28 cast-on, increasing to 30 cast-ons around the bottom, then decreasing to 28 cast-ons on the other side.

stitched leaves around each rose using the No 20 chenille needle. Couch in stems where necessary. Work some leaves in each of the four green shades to give a light and dark effect. See Diagram 2 for the method of stitching the leaves and refer to the photograph above for suggested colour placement.

Referring to the pattern, draw in the buds with a fabric pen. See Diagram 3 for the sequence of working the buds. Work the centre petal to match the centre of the rose belonging to the bud. Add green fly stitch leaves on each bud. Then couch

the stems into a curve for a softer look.

Mark in where the forget-me-not flowers will be stitched. Thread one strand of cornflower blue Gossamer Mohair into a No 22 chenille needle. Work five or six Lazy Daisy petals. Thread a No 22 chenille needle with gold ribbon and stitch a single French Knot in the middle of each flower.

For the buds, work one or two Lazy Daisy petals.

Add some Lazy Daisy leaves around the forget-me-nots using one strand of Glory 167, in a No 22 chenille needle.

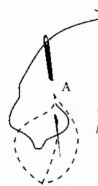

STEP 1: Bring needle and thread up at tip of leaf (A). Take needle down in front of A, bringing it up 5mm (¹/₄in) on the other side, keeping the thread underneath the needle.

STEP 2: Take a tiny stitch down at the centre of the leaf and come up beside the previous fly stitch.

STEP 3: Continue stitching, following the outline of the leaf until the shape is filled. Couch stems.

Diagram 2
Fly Stitch Leaves

MAKING UP

❖

When all the embroidery is finished, stretch it flat by spraying the back with water and nailing it onto a board. Leave to dry. If you have used a hoop, it may not be necessary to stretch the embroidery. If you have not already cut out the shape, do so now.

Also cut two layers of batting and the material for the lining. The tea-cosy shown has a double frill. For these, cut four 6cm (2¹/₂in) wide frill lengths of 140cm (1¹/₂yd), or double the length of the side seams of your tea-cosy. If you prefer a single frill, cut two lengths only. Fold the strips in half to make 3cm (1¹/₄in) wide frills.

Gather up the frills and stitch onto the sides of the blanketing. Cover the piping cord with lining fabric and stitch to the bottom of the cosy, curving it slightly around the corners on each side. Stitch one piece of batting to the wrong side of the blanketing, then tuck the other piece inside the stitched one.

Trim away the bulk and stitch the lining around three sides, leaving the bottom edge free. If the lining is too loose, add a dart down the centre to pull the excess in. Then turn right side out and hand stitch along the bottom edge to close. Cut the 24mm (1in) wide rose-coloured ribbon into 50cm (20in) lengths. Stitch one length of each colour together with a tiny seam across the width of the ribbon. Turn inside out and stitch again, enclosing the raw edges. Stitch onto the tea-cosy in between the double frill. The loose ends of the ribbon may be treated with a non-fray product if you wish.

Diagram 3
Stitching the Buds

Step 1: Using one strand of darkest colour, work first petal of 12 Cast-ons.

Step 2: Change to a lighter colour and work next petal of 8 Cast-ons, then another petal of 11 Cast-ons.

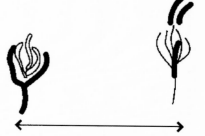

Step 3: Using one strand of green, stitch a Fly Stitch around the bud. Add two Straight Stitches in the centre of the bud and at the top.

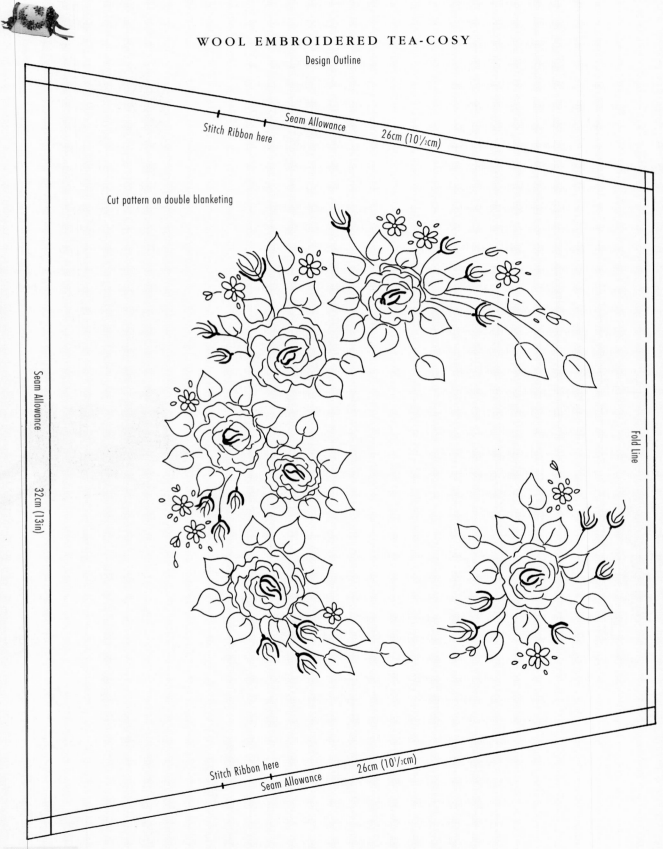

WOOL EMBROIDERED TEA-COSY

Design Outline

Stitch Ribbon here

Seam Allowance

26cm (10½cm)

Cut pattern on double blanketing

Seam Allowance

32cm (13in)

Fold Line

Stitch Ribbon here

Seam Allowance

26cm (10½cm)

 160%

Schwalm Handtowel

Traditional Schwalm embroidery is a combination of surface stitchery, pulled fabric, needleweaving, needlelace and drawn thread work. This design uses such familiar stitches as buttonhole, chain and satin stitch, while the lacy effect in the heart is worked in chequer filling stitch.

FINISHED SIZE

- 38cm x 69cm (15in x 27in)

MATERIALS

- 40cm x 70cm (16in x 28in) Permin antique pink 32-count linen
- No 12 DMC Flower Thread: one skein of ecru
- No 16 DMC Flower Thread: one skein of ecru
- Sewing thread to match fabric
- Contrasting light-coloured basting thread
- No 24 tapestry needle
- Adjustable embroidery frame or hoop
- Tracing paper
- Fine pencil

STITCHES USED

Coral Stitch, Chain Stitch, Chevron Stitch,
Buttonhole Stitch, Overcast Stitch,
Chequer Filling Stitch, Satin Stitch,
Ladder Stitch, Hemstitch

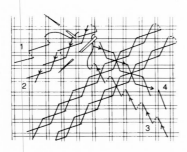

Chequer Filling Stitch

PREPARATION

Oversew the edges of the fabric by hand. Fold the fabric in half lengthways and, using coloured basting thread and running stitch, baste a line down the fold. Baste another line across the width of the fabric 15cm (6in) from the lower edge. See Diagram 1.

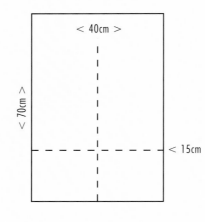

Diagram 1

Lightly transfer the outline of the design from the pattern on page 86 onto tracing paper with a fine pencil. Using running stitch and coloured thread, baste through both paper and the fabric, matching up the dotted line on the design with the basting lines on the fabric. When you have completely transferred the design, run a very sharp needle along the basting thread to perforate the paper. Carefully peel the paper away. Your design

is now transferred and you are ready to begin stitching. Mount the fabric in a frame with adjustable roller ends or use a round frame which can be removed when you have finished embroidering for the day.

EMBROIDERY

Commencing at point X and using No 16 Flower Thread, work Chain Stitch over two fabric threads inside the basting line of the inner heart. Remove the inner heart basting thread and, using No 12 Flower Thread, embroider Coral Stitch over two fabric threads around the outside of the Chain Stitch.

Still using No 12 Flower Thread, embroider Coral Stitch on the outside of the basting line around the outer heart. Remove the basting thread. Between the two rows of Coral Stitch, work Chevron Stitch in No 16 Flower Thread, commencing at the top of the heart. Chevron Stitch is usually embroidered in a straight line, however, to embroider it in a curve, space the outer stitches further apart than the inner stitches.

Outside the outer row of Coral Stitch, embroider Buttonhole Stitch semicircles using No 16 Flower Thread. As you can see from the design, the point and curves of the heart are accentuated. The centre filling is not worked until you have completed all the surface stitchery.

The small hearts either side of the centre motif are outlined first with chain

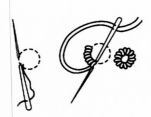

Overcast Eyelet

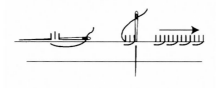

Hemstitch

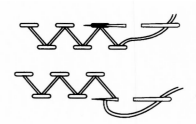

Chevron Stitch

stitch in No 16 Flower Thread, then Coral Stitch using No 12 Flower Thread outside that. The three-petal flower above the heart is embroidered using No 16 Flower Thread and Buttonhole Stitch. The eyelets are worked in No 16 Flower Thread and Overcast Stitch. All remaining design elements are embroidered with No 12 Flower Thread – the trailing stem and leaf outlines in Coral Stitch and the pods outlined with Coral Stitch and filled with Satin Stitch.

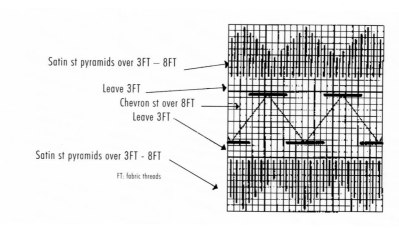

Diagram 3

DRAWN THREAD FILLING

The main heart shape is filled with Chequer Filling Stitch, which is worked over a grid of threads. To form the grid, leave the two threads marked on Diagram 2 and withdraw two threads, both warp and weft, either side of them (cut two fabric threads, leave two fabric threads, both horizontally and vertically).

Cut the threads as indicated and turn the fabric over to the wrong side. Withdraw the cut thread back to the edge with a blunt needle and cut the thread as close as possible to the edge. When you have completed the grid, embroider chequer filling stitch, beginning at point X, using No 12 Flower Thread.

Chequer Filling Stitch is worked diagonally across the grid, first one way, then the other, so that the two rows cross at right angles.

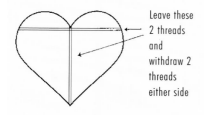

Diagram 2

For the first row, work from bottom left to top right and back to bottom left. Work the second row, bottom right to top left and back to bottom right.

As you are working within a curved edge you might not have sufficient space to embroider a whole Chequer Filling Stitch at the edge of all rows. When this occurs, work enough of the stitch to make sure the grid is covered and the design reads correctly. These stitches are called compensating stitches.

DECORATIVE BORDER

The border covers a total of thirty fabric threads and is placed ten threads below the base of the heart, leaving a 3cm (1¼in) wide hem allowance on both sides.

Use No 16 Flower Thread and begin the first row of Satin Stitch pyramids in the centre of the fabric, working out towards the hem allowance. Leave fourteen fabric threads and work the other side of the border with the satin stitch pyramids pointing down.

Between the two rows of pyramids, embroider Chevron Stitch over eight fabric threads, leaving three fabric threads top and bottom of the row. See Diagram 3.

MAKING UP

For the wide hem below the heart, mark two fold lines with a basting thread, the first forty-five horizontal fabric threads up from the edge and the second forty-seven fabric threads from this line. Then count up another fifty threads and withdraw a single thread. Fold and press down on the hem.

For the narrow top hem, withdraw one fabric thread 3cm (1¼in) from the edge and fold a 1cm (³⁄₈in) hem and press. Fold a 1cm (³⁄₈in) hem down both sides and hand-sew these sides first. Refold both top and bottom hems and pin in place. Carefully sew up the sides using ladder stitch and embroider hemstitch (working over three fabric threads) where the thread has been withdrawn on both hems.

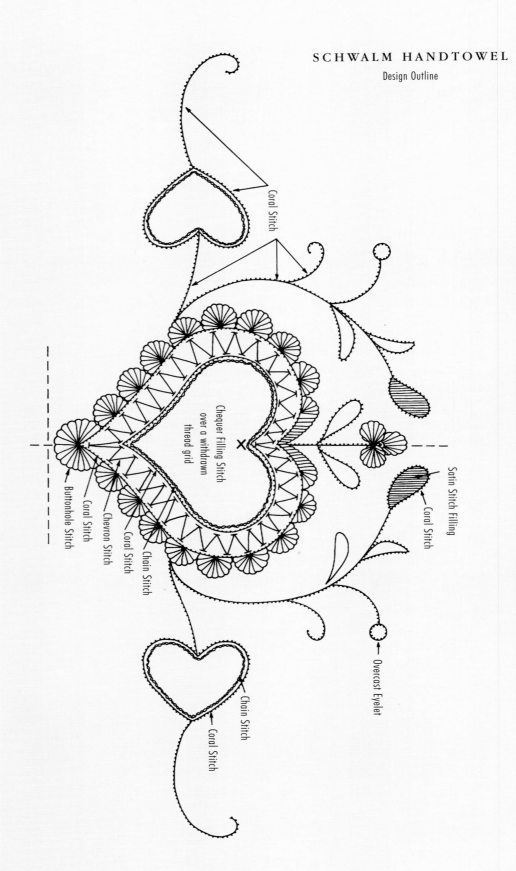

SCHWALM HANDTOWEL
Design Outline

Coral Stitch

Chequer Filling Stitch
over a withdrawn
thread grid

Satin Stitch Filling

Coral Stitch

Buttonhole Stitch

Coral Stitch

Chevron Stitch

Coral Stitch

Chain Stitch

Overcast Eyelet

Chain Stitch

Coral Stitch

125%

Antique Roses Cushion

Richly coloured ribbon roses on a dupion silk background
add romance and glamour to this beautifully decorative cushion.
The subtle shading of the roses is achieved
by blending the sheer and gradation ribbons together.

FINISHED SIZE

- 38cm (15in) square plus frill

MATERIALS

- 1.5m (1³/₈yd) main colour dupion silk
- 1.5m (1³/₈yd) contrasting colour dupion silk
- 23mm (⁷/₈in) Mokuba poly-rayon 4599: 3m (3¹/₄yd) beige (9), 2.5m (2³/₄yd) each of burgundy (15) and rust (10)
- 25mm (1in) Mokuba gradation rayon ribbon 4881: 8m (8³/₄yd) smoky brown (4)
- 25mm (1in) Mokuba graduation rayon ribbon 4882: 3m (3¹/₄yd) green (1)
- 15mm (⁵/₈in) Mokuba gradation rayon ribbon 4882: 1.5m (1⁵/₈yd) green (1)
- Mokuba 15mm (¹/₂in) crepe georgette ribbon 4546: 3m (3¹/₄yd) burgundy (66)
- YLI 4mm (¹/₄in) silk ribbon: 5m (5¹/₂yd) blue green (33), 3m (3¹/₄yd) green (21) and 4m (4³/₈yd) old gold (52)
- Marlitt thread: one skein each of tan (1001) and olive green (1011)
- Anchor Stranded Cotton: one skein of green (681)
- Stranded cottons to match roses
- No 13, 18 and 20 chenille needles
- No 3 and 7 milliners' needles
- Water-erasable fabric pen

STITCHES USED

Folded Ribbon Roses, Ribbon Stitch,
French Knots, Satin Stitch, Straight Stitch,
Stem Stitch, Bullion Stitch,
Lazy Daisy (Detatched Chain) Stitch,
Couching

NOTE: This is an inspirational project and no diagram is given. Follow the photograph for the positioning of the roses and buds, then place the other flowers in relation to them. You may choose to follow the design closely, or use it as a guide to create your own design.

PREPARATION

Cut a 43cm (17in) square of silk fabric. Overlock the edges to prevent fraying.

EMBROIDERY

Roses

Make seven folded ribbon roses (see Diagram 1 below) using the 23mm (⁷/₈in) poly-rayon ribbons in beige, burgundy and rust and the 25mm (1in) gradation ribbon in smoky brown (4). Using the poly-rayon ribbons and gradation ribbons together, make three roses in the beige and two roses each in the burgundy and rust.

Choose which way you want the cushion embroidered, that is on the straight or on the diagonal. With a water-erasable fabric pen, mark the corners of the cushion top fabric with rounded curves. Also mark the positions where the roses will be stitched.

When the roses are all completed, stitch them in place with matching coloured cotton thread.

Leaves

Using the No 13 needle, thread a 35cm (14in) piece of 25mm (1in) gradation rayon ribbon in green (1) and stitch the leaves in surrounding the roses with Ribbon Stitch. The stems are stitched in Stem Stitch with two strands of green (681) stranded cotton and the milliners' No 7 needle.

Finish off the loose ribbons at the back of the work with the stranded cotton.

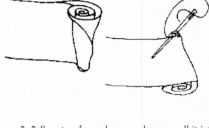

1. Fold raw edge down a little then roll ribbon three or four times to form centre of rose. Secure with three or four stitches.

3. Pull centre of rose down so when you roll it into the ribbon it will be level with the top of the fold. Stitch the base of the rose after each fold.

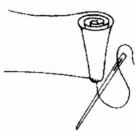

2. Fold ribbon on the cross. Each fold of ribbon is a petal.

4. Keep folding and stitching until you have the size and shape you want. To finish, stitch the ribbon at the bottom of the rose to prevent fraying.

Diagram 1 - Folded Ribbon Roses

Buds

Choosing ribbons to match the rose, make a couple of buds in each colour. Fold the two ribbons together, keeping the sheer ribbon on the outside. Cut the two ribbons 18cm (7in) long, hold the short ends in the right hand and fold the long side over the short. With your needle and matching thread, work gathering stitch across the base of the bud, pull the thread up and secure with a couple of stitches, then wrap the thread around the gathers two or three times.

Turn the bud to the back, with the open hood facing you. Fold the tail of the ribbon up into a roll, fold the roll in half and stitch it together. Then stitch a Running Stitch around the edge of the hood, push the rolled piece inside, and pull the gathers in tight and anchor. This will hold the centre piece in place. Now stitch the finished rosebud in place on the fabric.

Add some 15mm (³/₄in) gradation rayon ribbon in green (1) around each bud, using a No 18 chenille needle and wrapping it from side to side.

Blossom Flowers

With a No 13 needle, threaded with 35cm (14in) of burgundy crepe georgette ribbon (66), stitch five Ribbon Stitch petals, leaving a small centre. Fill the centre with French Knots in 4mm (¹/₈in) old gold silk ribbon (52). Scatter a few more French Knots around the centre ribbon ones, with two strands of tan Marlitt (1001) in a milliners' No 3 needle.

Blossom Buds

Mark the placement for the rosebuds, curving outwards from the flowers. Thread a No 13 chenille needle with 35cm (14in) of burgundy crepe georgette ribbon (66) and stitch in two Ribbon Stitches, side by side, very close together.

With two strands of tan Marlitt (1001) in a milliners' No 3 needle, add French Knots until the top is covered. Sew in the stems with two strands of green stranded cotton (681), curving the stems slightly towards the roses.

Bullion Sprays

With a No 3 milliners' needle and two strands of tan Marlitt thread (1001), stitch the flower heads with a ten-wrap Bullion Stitch. Work two to three Bullions, close together, for each flower, working them in a fan shape. Add the stems in Straight Stitch with two strands of olive green Marlitt (1011).

Forget-me-nots

Add a few forget-me-nots with 4mm (1/8in) old gold silk ribbon (52), threaded in a No 18 chenille needle, stitching five Ribbon Stitch petals for each flower.

Add a French Knot centre and some Lazy Daisy leaves using two strands of olive green Marlitt (1011).

Add a stitch with 4mm (1/8in) green silk ribbon (21) either side of the buds and one up the middle. Continue stitching in the stems, couching as you go.

Fern Leaves

Thread a No 20 chenille needle with 4mm (1/8in) blue-green silk ribbon (33). Draw the shape of the leaves with a fabric pen. Bring the ribbon tip halfway down the vein of the leaf. Straight-stitch, alternating to the left and the right until the leaf is complete, in the same way you would if you were working Satin Stitch in thread.

Spent Rose Heads

Thread a No 18 chenille needle with the 15mm (5/8in) wide gradation rayon ribbon in green (1) and Straight-stitch five petals facing downwards. With two strands of green stranded cotton (681), add Straight Stitches from the top of the petals.

FINISHING

When the embroidery is complete, make up the cushion with two contrasting frills cut on the cross. The cushion pictured has frills with finished widths of 8cm (3in) and 10cm (4in).

White Cats Needlework Set

Any cat-loving embroiderer will want to make this charming appliquéd and embroidered set of needlebook, pincushion and scissors case with scissors tassel. The cat appliqués could also be used to decorate a blouse pocket, a little girl's dress or whatever else your imagination suggests.

MATERIALS

- 30cm x 115cm (^{1}/$_3$yd x 45in) dupion silk in colour of your choice
- 25cm x 18cm (10in x 7in) cream silk for appliqué
- 25cm x 18cm (10in x 7in) fusible webbing
- 25cm x 18cm (10in x 7in) Pellon
- 12cm x 19cm (5in x 7^1/$_2$in) cream flannel
- DMC Stranded Embroidery Cotton: one skein each of white and light grey; four skeins of colour to match your dupion silk
- Sheet of template plastic
- 50cm x 7mm (20in x ^{1}/$_4$in) double-sided satin ribbon to match dupion silk
- Five pearls and a pearl button
- Small amount of stuffing for pincushion
- Sharp pencil
- Pinking shears
- Twisted cord to match dupion silk
- 5 silk tassels to match dupion silk

STITCHES USED

Back-Stitched Spider's Web, Cross Stitch, Fly Stitch, French Knot, Stem Stitch

PREPARATION

From the silk dupion cut: one piece 25cm x 19cm (10in x 7^1/$_2$in) for the needlebook; one piece 42cm x 13cm (16^1/$_2$in x 5^1/$_8$in) for lining; one piece 19cm x 13cm (7^3/$_8$in x 5^1/$_4$in) for lining; two pieces 14cm (5^1/$_2$in) square for the pincushion; one piece 24cm x 12cm (9^1/$_2$in x 5in) for the scissors case.

EMBROIDERY

On the needlebook piece, baste a line down the centre of the longest side. On the right hand side, 2cm (1in) in from the edges, mark dots with a sharp pencil for the centres of the flowers shown in the embroidery outline on page 95.

Work the flowers in Backstitched Spider's Web with three strands of white embroidery cotton. Refer to stitch diagram below. Make the corner flower the largest, with six spokes 4mm (^{1}/$_8$in) and stitch four times around the spokes. The next two flowers each side are a little smaller and stitched around three times, while the next two flowers are smaller again and stitched twice around. The last flower is worked on a tiny cross stitch with only one stitch on each leg.

With one strand of white cotton, work pairs of fly stitches around the flowers, then tip each Fly Stitch spoke with a French Knot in two strands of the main colour you have chosen.

Work similar sprays in the corners of one of the pincushion squares, but with only five flowers in each corner.

Fold the scissors case piece in half lengthwise and press. Then fold in half across the width and press.

Open out and on the lower right-hand quarter work small sprays of one medium flower as well as two small ones.

APPLIQUE

Back the cream silk with fusible webbing. Trace the cats onto the cream silk with dressmakers' carbon, and a sharp pencil to give you fine lines.

Cut out the cats very carefully, exactly on the outlines. Iron into position on each piece of the set.

With two strands of grey cotton, work stem stitch around the outlines, as close as possible to the edge of the applique. Work the details of the cats' faces and whiskers with one strand of grey.

MAKING UP

Needlebook

On the 42cm x 13cm (16^1/$_2$in x 5in) lining piece, make three 4cm (1^3/$_8$in) deep pleats, one underneath the other, and starting from one end of the 13cm (5^1/$_8$in) width. Press, then machine-stitch down the side edges and down the centre to form the pockets for the needlebook. Join this piece to the 19cm x 13cm (7^1/$_2$in x 5^1/$_4$in) lining piece. Press towards the plain side.

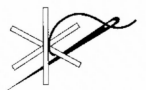

Lay a foundation of six evenly spaced spokes in a circle. Bring the needle and thread up near the centre and go back over one spoke and under two, repeating around all spokes until the circle is filled.

Back-stitched Spider's Web

Cut a piece of the Pellon to fit the embroidered side of the needlebook and attach it behind the embroidery with a few small stitches, taking care that the stitches do not show on the front of your work.

With right sides together, machine-stitch the lining to the embroidered piece around the sides and top only with a 1cm (³⁄₈in) seam. Leave the lower edge open. Then trim the seams and corners, turn right side out and press carefully under a cloth.

Cut two pieces of template plastic to fit the front and back of the needlebook. This will need to be measured carefully and a fraction of space left between the two sides to allow the book to fold easily.

Insert the plastic into the front and hand sew down the centre back, close to the plastic. Insert the plastic into the back, fold in the lower edge and oversew together with tiny stitches so the fabric is firm over the book.

Neaten the flannel with pinking shears and sew into the inside front with French Knots at 2cm (³⁄₄in) intervals, using four strands of thread of your chosen main colour.

Sew twisted cord around the edges (see instructions following), starting at the centre of the lower edges and leaving a loop for fastening at the centre right-hand edge.

Tie the 7mm (¹⁄₄in) satin ribbon around the centre back of the book and sew to secure. Tie a bow and secure it with a few invisible stitches. Stitch a pearl button on the opposite side to the loop.

Pincushion

Cut a piece of Pellon to fit the pincushion piece and attach it behind the embroidery. With right sides together, machine-stitch the two halves of the pincushion together with a 1cm (³⁄₈in) seam and leaving a 5cm (2in) opening on

one side. Trim the seams and corners, turn right side out and press under a cloth.

Fill with batting until the pincushion is well stuffed, then slip stitch the opening together.

Sew twisted cord around the seam starting at a back corner. Make or attach the ready-made four simple tassels and sew one to each corner with a pearl.

Scissors Case

With right sides together fold the scissors case piece in half across the narrower width and machine-stitch around the sides and top only, with a 1cm (³⁄₈in) seam. Leave the lower edge open. Trim the seams and corners, turn right side out and press.

Cut two pieces of template plastic to fit the front and back of the case.

cord for this set has three six-strand lengths of thread. The easiest method is to make the cord on the sewing machine. Knot one end of the strands to be twisted. Pass the other end through a hole in the machine bobbin and tie.

Hold the strands up from the bobbin and engage the bobbin winder. When little curls start to appear in the threads near the bobbin it is twisted enough.

Bring the two ends together, then let the threads twist together, giving the length a pull to even out the twists. Cut from the bobbin and tie an overhand knot in the end of the cord. To neaten the end, sew the end together with a needle and thread, then wrap the thread tightly around the end several times, and finish off. Cut the cord close to the wrapped end.

MAKING
A SIMPLE TASSEL

You need stranded cotton and a small piece of card 5cm (2in) wide.

Wind the thread 20 times around the card. Thread about 30cm (12in) of thread in a needle and take it between the wrapped strands and the cardboard at the top of the tassel. Firmly tie two overhand knots at the top.

Take the tassel off the card. To form the head, tie about 30cm (12in) of thread around the tassel about 1cm (³⁄₈in) from the top.

Turn the tassel over and tie again, then wind one end of the thread around the tassel several times, thread the end in a needle and take through the centre of the tassel. Repeat with the other end of the thread.

The threads left at the top of the tassel can be used to thread a bead and attach the tassel.

Insert the plastic and fold in lower edges. Oversew together with tiny stitches. Fold the case over and oversew the side and lower edges. Sew twisted cord around the sides and lower edge. Start at one side of the top, poking the end of the cord inside the case to secure. Finish at the other side in the same way. Take an 18cm (7in) length of cord and join into a loop. Make or attach a tassel (see instructions) over the join.

MAKING A
TWISTED CORD

For every strand of the cord, you need three times the finished length. The

WHITE CATS NEEDLEWORK SET
Appliqué Outlines

Embroidery Outline

Fuchsia Hot-water Bottle Cover

This wool and ribbon embroidered hot-water bottle cover
is a wonderful way to warm up chilly nights.
Using a combination of ribbon, wool and rayon threads,
the fuchsias are created with a variety of stitches.

PREPARATION

No pattern for the actual cover is given as hot-water bottles may vary in size. Fill your bottle and check your own measurements, allowing a little extra all round for both ease of fit and seam allowance. Draw a template to your measurements. Using any small round object, round off the corners.

Place the template onto your wool fabric, then mark the outline with a water-erasable pen or by basting with a contrast thread. Draw a matching front and back piece. The design outline is shown on page 98. It is not necessary to transfer the entire design – just the stems, bell shapes of the fuchsia and dots to indicate the tips of the leaves. Use a sunlit window if you can see through your fabric. Alternatively, you can use a transfer pencil or running stitch in a contrast thread. Then centre the design on the template.

EMBROIDERY

Use one strand of Gumnut Yarns and a double strand of DMC Médicis throughout. The fuchsias are not all worked in the same way. The letters A to E on the Colour Guide indicate method of working and colour variations. Refer to the table on page 99 for specific yarns and colours.

Work the fuchsia top petals first, then the lower petals and stamens. Next, work the stems, buds and leaves. All stamens are worked in straight stitch with a French knot at the tip of each. Work a double-wrap French Knot for the centre stamen and single-wrap for the side stamens. The buds are worked in Straight Stitch or Lazy Daisy filled with Straight Stitch. The stems are Straight Stitch.

The silk ribbon leaves are worked in Ribbon Stitch, single for the smaller leaves and two side Ribbon Stitches worked close together for the larger leaves. For side Ribbon Stitches, instead of piercing the ribbon in the centre, pierce to one side so the ribbon curls on one side only. Have the curls facing towards each other.

Fuchsias A and E
The top petals are Lazy Daisy filled with Straight Stitches. The bell-shaped lower petals are outlined in straight stitch forming a triangle, then filled with Straight Stitch. The stamens are worked in Straight Stitch with one strand of DMC Rayon Floss. Place a French Knot at the end of each Straight Stitch.

Fuchsias B
Work the top and bottom petals in Lazy Daisy filled with Straight Stitch. Work stamens as before.

Fuchsias C and D
Work the top and bottom petals in Straight Stitches. Stamens as before.

MAKING UP

In the centre of the bottom edge of the back piece, cut out a small half-moon shape to allow for the tab on the base of the bottle. Cut shallow scoops in the corners at the top of the back. See Diagram 1. Cut lining pieces to match front and back. Stitch lining to flannel, wrong sides together. Cut bias strips from the lining fabric for binding. Bind the half-moon shape on the back piece and then across the top of the back and out to the side seams. Place the lined sides together and bind the front and back pieces together. Finally, work two buttonholes at the top of the front piece and stitch buttons to wrong side of the back.

FINISHED SIZE
• 33cm x 26.5cm (13in x 10½in)

MATERIALS
• 30cm (12in) doctor's flannel
• 30cm (12in) cotton print lining fabric
• Gumnut Yarns Gemstones wool: one skein each of pinks (Ruby 1) and (Ruby 3)
• Gumnut Yarns Blossoms wool: one skein each of pinks (051) and (054); mauve (273); greens (576) and (597)
• DMC Medicis wool: one skein each of hot pinks (8685) and (8155); purples (8895) and (8794)
• DMC Rayon Floss: one skein each of pinks (30603) and (30915)
• No 3 crewel needle or No 22 chenille needle
• YLI silk ribbon: 2m x 7mm (2¼yd x ¼in) dark green (61), 3m x 7mm (3⅜yd x ¼in) light green (18)
• Embroidery hoop or frame (optional)
• Two buttons
• Water-erasable pen

STITCHES USED
Lazy Daisy (Detached Chain) Stitch,
Straight Stitch, French Knot, Ribbon Stitch,
Side Ribbon Stitch

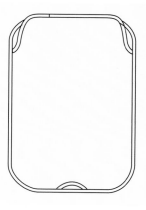

Diagram 1
Cut outs for cover back

FUCHSIA HOT-WATER BOTTLE COVER
Design Outline

FUCHSIA HOT-WATER BOTTLE COVER
Colour Guide

	FUCHSIA A	FUCHSIA B	FUCHSIA C	FUCHSIA D	FUCHSIA E
Top petals and buds	Blossoms (054)	Médicis (8794)	Médicis (8685)	Médicis (8155)	Blossoms (051)
Lower petals	Médicis (8895)	Blossoms (273)	Gemstones (Ruby 1)	Gemstones (Ruby 3)	Blossoms (054)
Stamens	DMC Rayon (30603)	DMC Rayon (30915)	DMC Rayon (30915)	DMC Rayon (30603)	DMC Rayon (30915)
Stems	Blossoms (597)	Blossoms (597)	Blossoms (576)	Blossoms (576)	Blossoms (576)
Leaves	YLI ribbon (18)	YLI ribbon (18)	YLI ribbon (61)	YLI ribbon (61)	YLI ribbon (18)

Purr-fectly Irresistible

This pampered Persian pussycat can be made as simple or as intricate as you like. In our photograph, the design is stitched on organza over calico then mounted in a rich velvet cushion, opulently braided and fringed.

PREPARATION

Transfer the basic design on page 103 onto calico using an iron-on transfer pencil. If you wish to trace the design directly onto calico using dressmakers' carbon paper, first place the design outline face down on a light box or other light source such as a window pane and trace the image onto paper before transferring the design to the calico. Place the organza over the top of the traced calico and secure in an embroidery hoop.

STITCHING

This is an inspirational project and there are no hard and fast directions for completing the cat embroidery. The basic design is the starting point. How much or how little additional embroidery you wish to add is a matter of personal preference.

Using Copper (1526), outline the basic design with a running stitch. Using Sapphire Blue (1443), whip the running stitch. Backstitch around the outline of the petal shape clusters and then work satin stitch over the backstitching.

Work the nine clusters shown on the basic design. These give the foundation on which you will build the further stitches. You can choose to follow the Colour Guide shown on page 102, working Lazy Daisy, Bullion Stitch, French Knots, Straight Stitch and Back Stitch as indicated, or create your own embellishment.

You will see from the coloured diagram that the areas around the face and the middle of the body have been only lightly embroidered to allow the organza to show through.

The French Knots vary between two twists and four twists. Estimate the length of your Bullion Stitches by wrapping your

thread closely around the needle. The length of the close wrapping on the needle should be equal to the length of the stitch. The longer Bullion Stitches which curve around the Satin Stitch petals may need to be held in place with a Couching Stitch.

The aim is to create an interesting texture and a feeling of opulence with the blending of the various shades. Have fun creating your very own Purr-fectly Irresistible embroidery!

MAKING THE CUSHION

Once completed, your embroidery can be mounted into a cushion, as shown here, or framed.

To mount into a cushion, cut four 10cm (4in) strips of velvet for the border. Baste or pin each side strip to the square of embroidered organza. Sew together. Then take the two remaining strips and attach them to the top and bottom of the square in the same way.

Attach the gold twisted cord to the seam joins, using a secure stitch. Sew the zipper in the centre back of the cushion. With right sides together, sew the cushion front to the back. Turn right way out.

Place the insert inside the cushion. Stitch the edging braid around the cushion edge seams. Attach the tassels securely at even intervals.

FINISHED SIZE

- Approximately 40cm (16in) square

MATERIALS

- 25cm (10in) square organza
- 25cm (10in) square calico
- Approximately 50cm (20in) velvet or velveteen for border strips
- Approximately 50cm (20in) square fabric for cushion back
- Rayon thread: gold, pale gold, sapphire blue, pearl, dark gold, medium gold, copper, olive green
- Size 10 quilter's needle
- Iron-on transfer pencil or dressmakers' carbon paper
- Embroidery hoop
- Zipper to fit cushion
- Cushion insert to fit
- Decorative edging braid
- Gold twisted cord
- Tassels (optional)

STITCHES USED

Lazy Daisy (Detached Chain) Stitch,
Bullion Stitch, French Knots, Satin Stitch,
Back Stitch, Straight Stitch

NOTE: Experience is necessary to complete this embroidery project as photographed. The embroidery is worked throughout with one strand. The Design Outline shown on page 103 has been given in reverse to make it easy when using an iron-on transfer pencil.

PURR-FECTLY IRRESISTIBLE
Colour Chart

STITCH KEY

Satin Stitch

Lazy Daisy Stitch

French Knot

Bullion Stitch

— — — — Straight Stitch

· · · · · · Back Stitch

COLOUR KEY

gold

pale gold

sapphire blue

pearl

dark gold

medium gold

copper

olive green

PURR-FECTLY IRRESISTIBLE
Design Outline — Shown Reversed

Smocked Summer Dress

Any square-yoke dress pattern is suitable for this design, which transforms a simple summer dress into something unique. It is smocked using Rajamahal Art Silk thread and cable and wave stitch combinations.

GENERAL INSTRUCTIONS

This design suits any dress pattern on a square yoke. The fabric used in the photograph is probably no longer available, but the style is so simple that it can easily be adapted to any fabric and colour. Don't be frightened to experiment!

Study the fabric. It will have a definite background colour, which will become the colour of the insert. Use a fine cotton, linen or poly-cotton that has a high percentage of cotton in it.

Using a plain insert enables you to choose your colours for smocking with more freedom; you don't need the design and colours to be heavy to be seen as the contrast in colours is sufficient.

No 6 or 7 crewel needles may be larger than you are used to, but you will find there is less wear and tear on the threads if you use the larger sized needles.

PREPARATION

As the Rajmahal threads are 100 per cent viscose, you may find it necessary to 'wax' them before use.

Dissolve about a quarter of a bar of pure soap to one litre (2 pints) of cold water. Untwist each skein of thread but don't unwind it.

Wet the thread in the liquid and allow it to dry on a clean towel.

The thread will be waxed evenly. Once the thread is dry, wind it onto a cardboard cylinder.

On completion of your work, if the thread's lustre has not returned with handling, rinse it in a solution of light white vinegar and water. This will set the colours as well as returning the lustre to the threads.

INSERT

Centre your fabric by folding it in half and creasing lightly with a fingernail. With a strong contrasting colour from outside your colour scheme, run a line of basting stitch down the crease. This makes working much easier, as your pattern can be centred without tedious counting and the finished piece is already marked ready for insertion into the yoke and skirt. The basting thread is removed at the end.

There are two good reasons why you should not pleat from seam to seam: first comfort for the wearer and the prevention of wear on the threads; second to form a frame around the work, enhancing the design. Place small marks about 7.5cm (3in) from each end of the fabric. The pleating will be between these two points. Pleat up 12 rows. This gives two Holding Rows which are not shown on the graph page 107. Pull threads back to the pre-marked lines. Tie the threads off to the desired width. Steam the piece heavily and allow to cool and dry.

SMOCKING

Start at the centre and work out. This saves wear on the threads and ensures the pattern is always centred. Do not tie off the embroidery threads for the first couple of rows so you can easily subtract or add pleats to suit until the pattern is established.

The first cable/wave combination is shown in black on the graph on page 107. The diamonds and half-diamonds are worked next and are shown in blue. The satin stitch is shown in red.

Begin at the centre of Row 2 (using long threads as you will be working out to both ends – there are no knots). Start

MATERIALS

- Square yoke dress pattern
- Floral fabric (amount required for pattern)
- 15cm x 115cm (6in x 45in) of plain fabric for insert
- Rajmahal Art Silk thread: one skein each of Spring Leaf (152), Hot Orange (235), Winter White (90), Wheat Gold (91), Moroccan Gold (94), Vermilion (255)
- No 6 or 7 crewel needles

STITCHES USED

Cable, Five-Cable and Full-Step Wave combination, Full-Step Wave, Half-Step Wave or Baby Wave, Satin Stitch

with the (black) over cable on the centre pleat, follow the graph and complete another two cables, then step down one full row and stitch the five-cable combination, commencing with an under cable. This is followed by a full step up and another five-cable combination, starting with an up cable. Continue to the end. Turn work upside down and complete other side.

Starting at the centre of Row 4 and commencing with an under cable, follow the smocking graph.

Start at the centre of Row 4 with an over cable and follow the graph.

Start at the centre of Row 7 with an under cable and follow the graph.

Start at the centre of Row 7 with an over cable and follow the graph.

Start at the centre of Row 9 with an under cable and follow the graph.

This completes the framework or background.

Diamonds and half-diamonds are worked between the framework. Beginning your work on the left side, work the diamond/half diamond and

Half diamonds between Rows 4 and 5 and Rows 6 and 7 are worked in two strands of Wheat Gold (91) and two strands of Moroccan Gold (94).

Between Rows 5 and 6, in four strands of Moroccan Gold (94), work two rows of baby wave commencing at the centre. Follow the graph.

Work two Satin Stitches in each of the small diamonds, following the graph.

Start at the centre of Row 1 and work a row of cable commencing with an over cable. Follow the graph.

Starting at centre of Row 10, work a row of cable commencing with an under cable. Again, follow the graph.

The Holding Rows are not seen on the completed garment but are very important. They give the insert stability during construction. On these two rows you can work either a row of cable which is a mirror of the first row and Row 10, or an Outline or Stem Stitch. The choice is yours. The only rule is that these two rows must be worked right at the top of the pleat.

Your design is now complete. The design looks simple but you do need to be careful if colour grading.

then carry the thread across the back by doing cable stitches right at the top of the pleat.

The half-diamonds are worked first in four strands of Winter White (90) between Rows 2 and 3. The stitch combination is an over cable, one full-step wave down, an under cable, a full-step wave up and an over cable. Between Rows 8 and 9 the half diamonds are reversed, giving a mirror image.

The first group of diamonds is worked in three strands of Winter White (90) and one strand of Wheat Gold (91) between Rows 2 and 4 and Rows 7 and 9. These are a combination of single-cable and wave.

The second lot of diamonds are worked in one strand of Winter White (90) and three strands of Wheat Gold (91) between Rows 3 and 5 and Rows 6 and 8.

✄ HELPFUL HINT

Fabrics should be washed before pleating. This will help realign the grain and remove any sizing. A rinse in a fabric conditioner will help soften the fabric to make pleating easier.

SMOCKING GRAPH

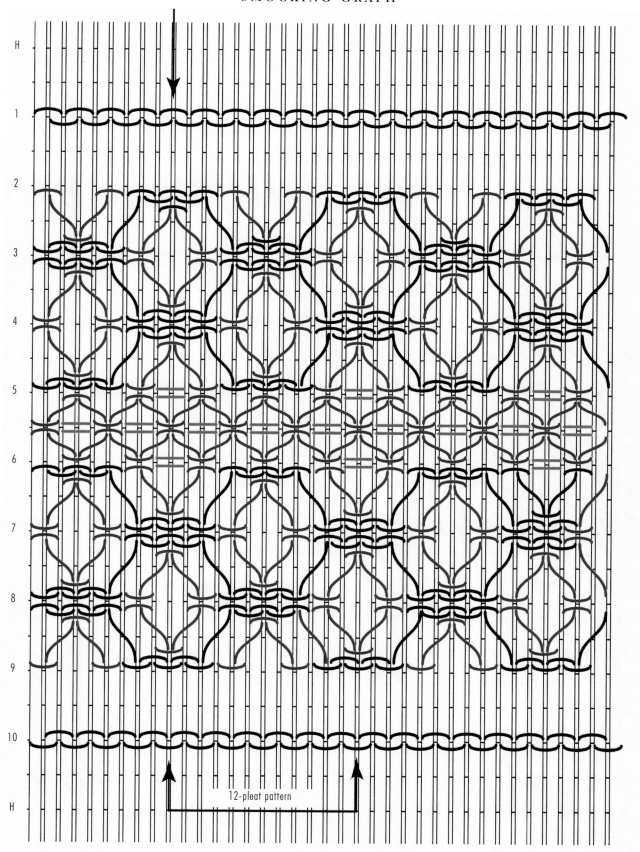

12-pleat pattern

Heavenly Hardanger

The perfect companions for fine dining, these placemats and matching coasters were worked using thread that is hand-dyed pure silk (equivalent to a Coton Perlé No 8) which pulls smoothly through the even-weave fabric, without showing signs of wear.

PREPARATION

The graphs given on pages 112-113 give one quarter of each design.

The graph lines represent the evenweave fabric threads and the heavy lines represent the embroidery threads.

Overlock the edges of the fabric squares or run a thin line of fray stopping liquid around the edge to prevent fraying while embroidering. Using contrasting thread, baste the vertical and horizontal centre lines on each piece of fabric. These basting lines will correspond with the centre lines marked on the pattern.

The stitching must be done in strict order. Starting from the centre, all the satin stitching is completed first, then the back stitching, colonial knots and finally the buttonhole edging. Do not cut the edge until all the embroidery has been completed.

Using an embroidery hoop will help to keep an even tension on your work and avoid puckering the fabric.

STITCHING PLACEMATS

Cut a length of thread no longer than 38cm (15in). Thread into the needle and knot the end. Take the needle through the right side of the fabric approximately 8cm (3¼in) from the starting point and come up from the back at A to start stitching. When you wish to finish off the thread run it under the satin-stitching or buttonhole-edging two or three times on the wrong side, catching the fabric threads with the needle. Then go back to the beginning of the thread. Cut the knot, thread the needle and finish off in the same way. This process is called a waste knot. A new waste knot should be used for each thread of the embroidery. To finish the thread for the back

stitching, run the thread in and out of the stitching on the back of the embroidery until it is secure.

From the point where the two basting lines meet, count out two threads to A. This will be the starting point for the satin stitch.

Using medium pink (194), work all the satin stitch motifs. See Diagram 1. On the front of the work the satin stitches should lie on the same horizontal line. On the back of the work the stitches should be slightly slanted and there should be no tiny vertical stitches.

Change to dark pink (196) and embroider the backstitching and then work the colonial knots where indicated.

From the centre, count out 104 threads to B. This is the starting point for the border pattern. Using medium pink (194), Satin Stitch the first row of the border. When you reach a point where the stitching begins to go at right angles, the first stitch around the corner should start from the hole shared with the previous stitch.

There should not be a long diagonal stitch across the corner on the back of the work.

Next, work the backstitch and colonial knot border.

MATERIALS

(for two placemats and two coasters)

- Two x 41 cm (16in) squares cream 28-count even-weave fabric (for placemats)
- Two x 13cm (5in) squares cream 28-count even-weave fabric (for coasters)
- Gumnut Yarns silk thread: four skeins of medium pink (194), two skeins of dark pink (196)
- No 24 tapestry needle
- Embroidery scissors with fine, sharp blades and points
- Fray stopping liquid (optional)
- Embroidery hoop (optional)
- Contrasting thread

STITCHES USED

Satin Stitch, Back Stitch, Colonial Knot, Buttonhole Stitch

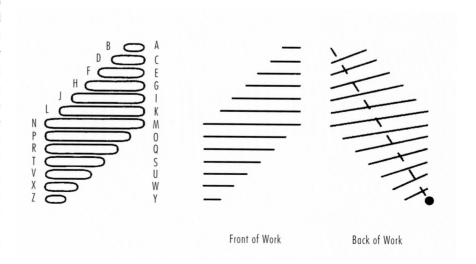

Front of Work   Back of Work

Diagram 1

Detail of the placemat embroidery.

The final embroidery step is the buttonhole edging. Work from left to right. See Diagrams 2 and 3.

To turn an outside corner, pivot the thread at B while counting two threads to the right of the last stitch and coming up at C. Take the needle in again at B and come out at D (two threads to the right of C). Turn the fabric 90 degrees, put the needle in again at B and come out at E (two threads to the right of D), in once more at B and out at F (two threads to the right of E). This completes the outside corner.

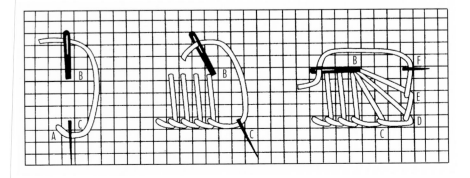

Diagram 2

Satin stitch according to the pattern until you reach the next (inside) corner. Turn the fabric so that your satin stitches are in a horizontal position. Bring the needle out at the base of the last and take a vertical stitch as shown in Diagram 3, working a buttonhole stitch into the same hole you started from.

CUTTING THE EDGE

When all stitching has been completed, it is time to cut the edge. Use your embroidery scissors and work from the wrong side of the embroidery. By working from the back you can get closer to the embroidered edge and prevent a fluffy-looking finish.

Now, slide the blade of the sharp scissors underneath a fabric thread on the outside edge of the buttonholing and cut it carefully, as close as you can to the embroidery.

It takes a while to work around the edge and care must be taken not to cut the embroidery thread.

When the cutting is complete, press on the wrong side of the embroidery with a warm iron.

STITCHING COASTERS

Starting at A, use medium pink thread (194) to Satin Stitch the centre motif. Using dark pink (196), work a colonial knot in the centre of the motif.

Count out 30 threads from the centre to B. Using dark pink (196), work the Back Stitch and Colonial Knot border.

Change to medium pink (194) and work the buttonhole edge. Cut around the edge as for placemat and press on the wrong side with a warm iron.

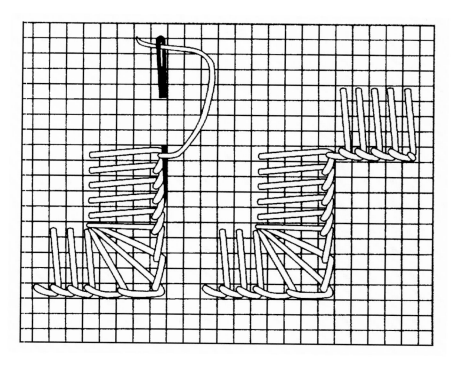

Diagram 3

HEAVENLY HARDANGER
Placemat
Graph

Back Stitch

Buttonhole Stitch

Colonial Knot

Satin Stitch

B

A

118%

HEAVENLY HARDANGER
COASTER
Graph

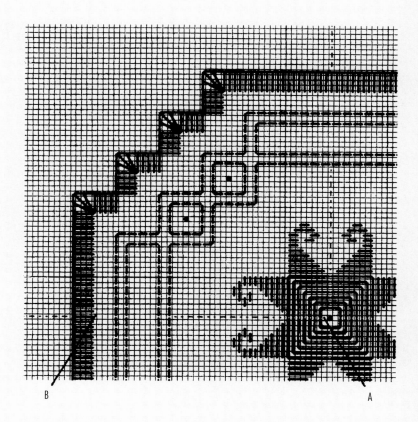

B   A

Great to Give or Get

There's nothing like a handmade gift to let people know you care, whether it's a delightful beaded pincushion or charming name plaques for a child's room. The only problem you're likely to have is that you will fall in love with these superb projects and be unable to part with them.

Crewel Tea Cloth

This delightful old-fashioned tea cloth is reminiscent of leisurely teas on summer afternoons with tea cakes, scones and dainty biscuits. In the style of embroidered cloths from early this century, the colourful floral design is worked in simple crewel stitches.

FINISHED SIZE

• 95cm (37½in) square

MATERIALS

• 1m (39½in) square piece of white linen (we used 20 threads per centimetre [50 threads per inch] DMC Kingston linen)

• Rajmahal Art Silk threads: one skein each of Tangier sand (44), baby camel (45), winter white (90), wheat gold (91), chardonnay (93), cinnamon (104), purple dusk (113), bluebell (121), cossack blue (122), royal blue (126), barely pink (200), dusky rose (241), hot plum (256), citrus sorbet (261), maidenhair (521); two skeins each of mango cream (141), peacock green (165), gentle magenta (181); three skeins of vibrant musk (184)

• Crewel needles

• Buttonhole twist cotton for hemming

• Water-erasable pen

• Tissue paper

• Sharp embroidery scissors

STITCHES USED

Long Stitch, Short Stitch, French Knots,

Chain Stitch, Stem Stitch, Straight Stitch

PREPARATION

Transfer the design onto paper. Using a water-erasable pen, transfer it onto the centre of the cloth, positioning two repeats in the centre, 20cm (8in) apart and in diagonal corners. Cut threads into lengths than 35cm (14in) and sort, coding them with colour numbers.

EMBROIDERY

Follow the design and detail picture for colour placement. Work the leaves and blue flowers. Stitch large areas on flowers in long and short stitch, yellow daisy centre in French Knots, leaf outlines in Chain Stitch and stems in Stem Stitch.

On large dark green leaves, stitch short veins with a single straight stitch. In the centre of the large magenta rose, work lines of definition in hot plum 256.

EDGING

Work a machine stitched scalloped hem around the cloth.

Mark a hemline to give a cloth 95cm (34in) square. Set your sewing machine to an automatic scallop stitch. Place a piece of tissue paper underneath the fabric, between fabric and feed dogs (the tissue helps fabric to feed through the machine). Stitch along the marked line. Tear tissue paper away and using sharp embroidery scissors, trim fabric next to the stitching.

CREWEL TEA CLOTH
Design Outline

110%

Beaded Pincushion

Even if you've never tried beading before, this gorgeous little pincushion will be irresistible. Only two simple stitches are used – cross stitch and half cross stitch for attaching the beads. It is worked with stranded cotton and antique beads, and finished with tassels.

DESIGN AREA

- 15cm (6in) square using 25-count linen (75 stitches square)

MATERIALS

- 30cm (12in) square 25-count linen
- 18cm (7in) square of fabric for cushion back
- DMC Stranded Embroidery Cotton: one skein each of dark green (500) and ecru
- Mill Hill Seed Beads: one packet each of Copper (0330) and Bronze (0221), two packets of Gold (557)
- Mill Hill Antique Beads: one packet each of Eggplant (3004), Antique Cranberry (3003), Midnight (3002), Cognac (3036)
- No 9 applique needle (for attaching beads)
- No 24 or 26 tapestry needle (for Cross Stitch)
- Four small tassels
- 20cm (8in) embroidery hoop (optional)
- Contrasting thread
- Polyester stuffing

STITCHES USED

Half Cross Stitch, Cross Stitch

PREPARATION

Overlock or hand overcast the raw edges of the linen to prevent fraying. Fold your fabric in half vertically and horizontally to find the centre.

Work a line of basting stitches from top to bottom through the centre and then work another line from side to side. Where the lines intersect is the centre of the fabric.

Each square on the graph represents two threads of fabric.

From the horizontal centre basting line, count up 53 threads and 55 threads to the left. This is the starting point for the first row of the central beaded panel. The outside border is worked last.

STITCHING

Counted bead embroidery is worked with a half cross stitch. The symbols on the chart indicate the colours of the beads to use. Work from left to right, beginning in the lower left corner of the stitch. To start a thread, leave a short tail at the back and secure by stitching the first few stitches over it. Bring the needle up in the appropriate position, thread on a bead and go back into the fabric two

threads to the right and two threads up. All stitches must go in the same direction to ensure that the beads sit properly on the fabric. Finish off the thread by weaving through several stitches on wrong side of work.

Attach the Antique Cranberry beads last, as this is a delicate colour.

Work the cross stitch in two strands of DMC dark green (500).

Work the beaded border after you finish the central panel.

FINISHING

Your completed piece may be washed in cool water and a mild soap. Place right side down on a towel to dry. While still damp, iron the piece dry. The use of an ironing aid such as Fabulon also improves the look of the finished work. Do not press too hard with the iron as it will distort the position of the beads.

MAKING UP

With contrasting thread, baste all around the embroidery, five threads out from the beading.

Trim linen to within 1cm (³/₈in) of the basting line. Catch the ends of the tassels in place at each corner, with the tassels facing inwards.

Place the embroidery and backing fabrics together, right sides facing and machine-stitch close to the basting lines. Trim seam allowance if necessary.

Leave a small opening for turning and stuffing. Turn to the right side and pull the corners and tassels out.

Fill the pincushion with polyester stuffing, then, using ecru thread, slip stitch the opening closed.

BEADED PINCUSHION
Graph

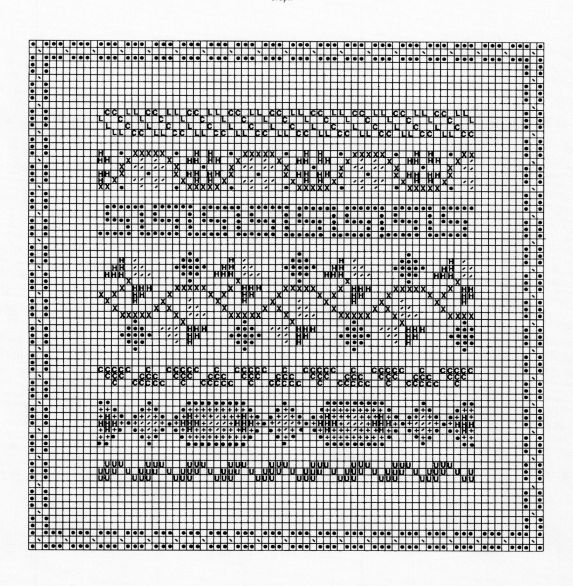

KEY
Mill Hill Beads

- ● = Gold (557)
- ✔ = Antique Cranberry (3003)
- H = Midnight (3002)
- c = Cognac (3036)
- + = Copper (0330)
- U = Eggplant (3004)
- L = Bronze (0221)

DMC Stranded Embroidery Cotton

- x = Dark Green (500)

His & Her Name Plaques

*What a great gift for a child! These delightful pink and blue name
plaques can be hung on a bedroom door or above a bed.
An alphabet is provided so you can personalise your design,
and even make one for the whole family!*

PREPARATION

Overlock or tape the raw edges of the fabric to prevent fraying. Find the centre of the fabric by folding in half vertically and horizontally. Run a line of basting stitches along the folds. The lines will intersect at the centre of the fabric. To find the corresponding centre of the design, use a pencil and ruler to join the arrows top to bottom and side to side.

Each square shown on the graph represents a cross stitch and each symbol represents the colour you should use.

STITCHING

The design is worked in cross stitch using two strands of cotton. For the back stitching, use two strands of either the cotton or the stranded metallic thread.

Separate the threads and allow to unwind before rejoining and threading into your needle. To begin a thread, bring the needle from the back of the fabric to the front, leaving a short tail of thread on the wrong side. Hold this tail against the fabric and secure with the first few

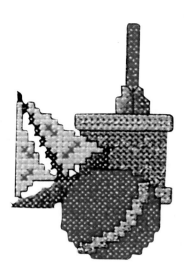

stitches. To end off threads, weave the thread through the back of several stitches to secure it. Working with an embroidery hoop or frame will give better tension, but do not leave the embroidery in the hoop when you are not working on it, as this may result in marks that are difficult to remove.

Start stitching at the centre of the graph. Complete the lettering and toys before stitching the border. It is important that all your stitches travel in the same direction. Refer to the Stitch Graphs for cross stitch illustration. When you have completed all the cross stitching, work the backstitching as indicated on the graph.

FINISHING

Before taking your completed work to be framed it is a good idea to freshen it up by washing it. Using warm water and a pure soap, swish the fabric gently through the water. Do not rub. Rinse it well and dry flat. Do not wring. To avoid flattening the stitches, place the completed cross stitch face down on a light-coloured, fluffy towel and press from the back with a warm iron.

FINISHED SIZE

• 30cm x 10cm (12in x 4in) (design only)

MATERIALS

• 45cm x 25cm (18in x 10in) piece of Zweigart 14-count, white Aida

• No 24 tapestry needle

• Embroidery hoop or frame (optional)

• Pencil, ruler

For the blue-toned design:

• DMC Stranded Embroidery Cotton: one skein each of black brown (3371), very dark beige brown (838), very dark pink/brown (632), medium pink/brown (3064), dark tan (437), very light tan (738), cream (712), light carnation (893), medium pink (776), dark pistachio green (367), light pistachio green (368), light Wedgwood (3760), sky blue (519) very light topaz (727)

• DMC Metallic Floss: gold (317.5282)

For the pink-toned design:

• DMC Stranded Embroidery Cotton: one skein each of black brown (3371), very dark beige brown (838), very dark pink/brown (632), medium pink/brown (3064), dark tan (437), very light tan (738), cream (712), dark blue (825), light blue (813), dark pistachio green (367), light pistachio green (368), dark Christmas red (498), bright Christmas red (666), very light topaz (727)

• DMC Metallic Floss: gold (317.5282)

STITCHES USED

Cross Stitch, Back Stitch

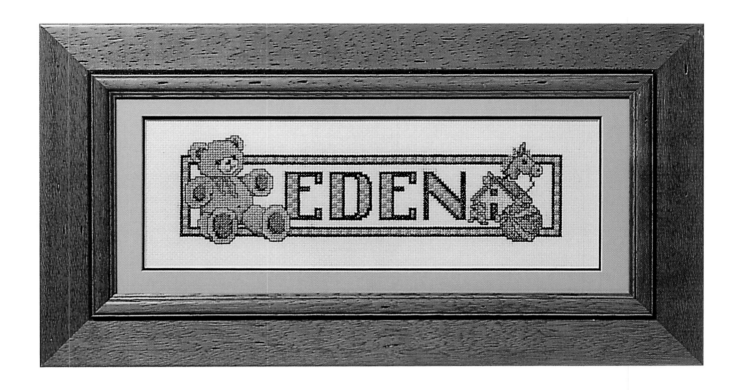

HIS & HER NAME PLAQUES
Alphabet Graph
(for colours, refer to plaque keys on page 126)

HIS & HER NAME PLAQUES
Stitch Graphs

Pink-toned design

Blue-toned design

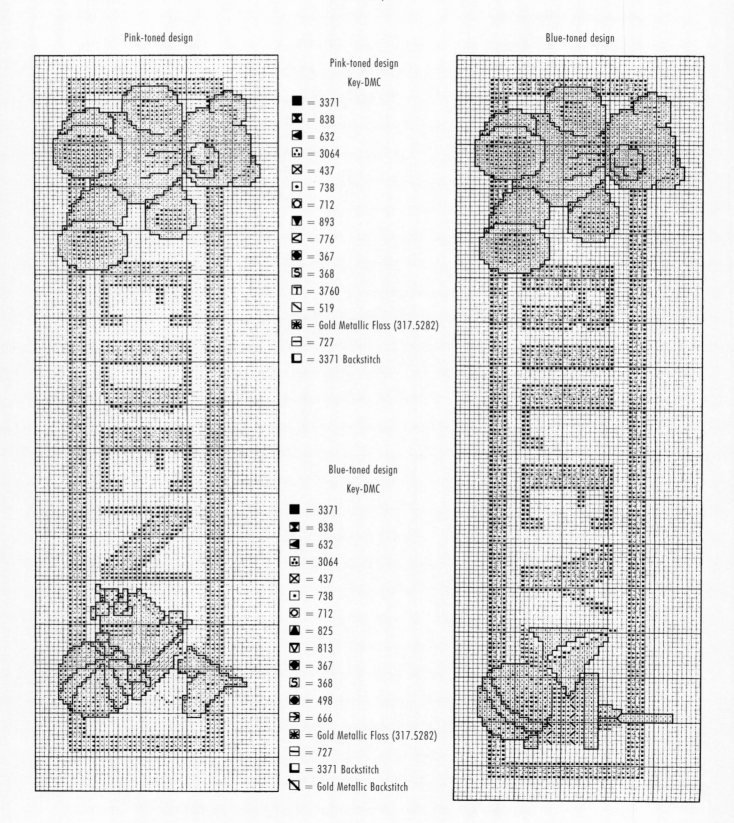

Pink-toned design
Key-DMC

■	=	3371
⬕	=	838
◧	=	632
⠿	=	3064
⊠	=	437
⊡	=	738
◎	=	712
▼	=	893
◩	=	776
⬢	=	367
⑤	=	368
⊞	=	3760
◨	=	519
✳	=	Gold Metallic Floss (317.5282)
⊟	=	727
◱	=	3371 Backstitch

Blue-toned design
Key-DMC

■	=	3371
⬕	=	838
◧	=	632
⠿	=	3064
⊠	=	437
⊡	=	738
◎	=	712
▲	=	825
▼	=	813
⬢	=	367
⑤	=	368
◕	=	498
⮞	=	666
✳	=	Gold Metallic Floss (317.5282)
⊟	=	727
◱	=	3371 Backstitch
◥	=	Gold Metallic Backstitch

Embroidered Handtowel

This elegant handtowel features a colourful cottage garden design and is finished with cream antique lace and burgundy satin ribbon. Stitched with stranded cotton, it makes a pretty addition to a Victorian-style bathroom.

MATERIALS

• Cream handtowel

• DMC Stranded Cotton: one skein each of light blue violet (341), very dark salmon (347), medium shell grey (452), very light old gold (677), medium old gold (729), light garnet (814), very dark garnet (902), very dark avocado green (936), dark khaki green (3011), medium khaki green (3012), light khaki green (3013), medium antique violet (3041), dark salmon (3328), medium salmon (3712), dark antique violet (3740), chocolate brown (3772), medium sportsman flesh (3773), very light sportsman flesh (3774)

• No 7 crewel needle

• 40cm x 7mm (16in x ¼in) burgundy ribbon

• 40cm x 5cm (16in x 2in) cream cotton lace

STITCHES USED

Stem Stitch, Bullion Stitch, Fly Stitch,

Lazy Daisy (Detached Chain) Stitch,

Buttonhole Stitch, Colonial Knot,

Blanket Stitch, Couching, Satin Stitch,

Straight Stitch

PREPARATION

Follow the design outline at the bottom of the page, stitching the main features first. All embroidery is worked in three strands unless otherwise stated.

EMBROIDERY

TOPIARY TREE

For the trunk, draw a straight line 35mm (1½in) long and Stem-stitch over it in 3011, then whip with 3013 to form the vine. Place three small grub roses above the trunk in an irregular triangular shape. To make each rose use Bullion Stitches with 347 and 3712.

Randomly place six or seven buds close to the grub roses. Fly-stitch around the buds in 3011 and join to the roses. Put two Lazy Daisy leaves either side. Place Lazy Daisy leaves all around to form an irregular circular shape for the tree using 3011 and 3012.

HOLLYHOCKS

Using 3041 thread, Buttonhole-stitch four circles, gradually getting smaller as you go up. Use 452 to place a Colonial Knot in

the centre of each and three at the end. Put a few Lazy Daisy leaves at the bottom and middle of the flower using 3011.

MIDDLE THREE HOLLYHOCKS

Again, Buttonhole-stitch circles, grading their sizes as per the diagram, using 3773, 3772 and 3013 for the leaves.

DAFFODILS

Using 3012, Stem Stitch leaves and stems, tilting stems at the top. Blanket-stitch trumpets of flower in 729, apart from the stems. Use a Lazy Daisy Stitch for the three petals in 677, with the middle petal overlapping the stem.

LAZY DAISY FLOWERS

Couch stems in 3013 and place Lazy Daisy leaves randomly up them. Work two half flowers with five petals in 3774 and one flower with six petals. Place a Colonial Knot in the centre using 729.

AGAPANTHUS

Work small Fly Stitches around in a circle using 341, leaving a gap in the bottom for the stems. Using one strand of 3011, work five to six Straight Stitches, half the Fly Stitch length.

Use Stem Stitch for stems with one strand of 3011 and two of 936. For the leaves, use rows of Stem Stitch beside each other, meeting at the top.

EMBROIDERED HANDTOWEL DESIGN

Enlarge or reduce pattern to fit across towel

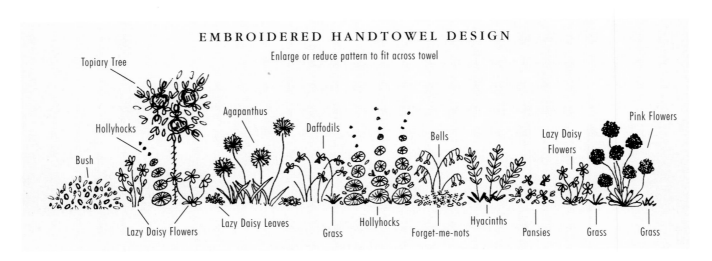

BUSH

Randomly place approximately seven buds in 814. Using 936, stitch Lazy Daisy leaves randomly to form a bush shape. Use Colonial Knots with one strand of 902 and two strands of 814 amongst leaves to give texture and colours.

BELLS

Work stems in Stem Stitch with one strand of 936 and two of 3011. Using 902, bring the needle up a short distance away from the stem and work a Lazy Daisy Stitch. Place two smaller Lazy Daisy Stitches on either side, having them face down. Leave some flowers with just one Lazy Daisy Stitch.

HYACINTHS

Using couching in 3011, place stems leaving a good size gap between each so as to not bunch them up. The flowers have been worked using Lazy Daisy Stitch in two strands of 3740 and one of 452. Place three petals together at top of stems then spread three or four more petals down either side of stems. Lastly, stitch the leaves in Satin Stitch.

LAZY DAISY FLOWERS – RIGHT OF TOPIARY TREE

Stitch Lazy Daisy flowers first using a variety of petals for full and half flowers in 3774 and 3773. Stitch Colonial Knots on centres using 3772. Couch stems in two strands of 3012 and one of 3013, being sure to curve them. Use Lazy Daisy stitches for the leaves.

RIGHT END PINK FLOWERS

Couch stems in 3012 making them larger than the flowers beside them but not as big as the topiary tree. Stitch lots of Colonial Knots close to each other to form the flowers. Use 3328 and 3712 on their own or mix strands together. Try and keep the light colour at the top of the bush and the darker colour at the

bottom. For the leaves at the base of the flowers use Lazy Daisy Stitches.

FORGET-ME-NOTS

These are a wonderfully simple flower to sew and are very effective and pretty. Randomly place centres of flowers in any space to be filled using Colonial Knots in 729 thread.

Around each centre knot stitch five or six more Colonial Knots close to each other in 341. Leaves are again filled in with Lazy Daisy Stitch.

PANSIES

This is a good flower to fill in spaces. Work in three Lazy Daisy petals using 902. Next, using 729, stitch three blanket stitches to form the bottom petals.

Randomly place these flowers close to one another and scatter Lazy Daisy leaves around them in 936, leaving them bare with no leaves.

Not every garden will be the same and no doubt there will be spaces left between flowers and where stems are spread out.

Try to fill these with small simple stitches to give a fuller effect or stitch grass in 936 using Straight Stitches in a few different patches.

In the larger spaces, randomly stitch Lazy Daisy leaves in a green cotton and place Colonial Knots over the top, either mixing the different coloured threads or the plain colour to match the ribbon and unite the garden.

ATTACHING RIBBON AND LACE

Thread the ribbon through the lace. Pin the lace in place on the towel under the stitched design and carefully stitch either side of the ribbon and down both sides, being sure to secure ends.

Garden Flowers Knee Rug

This cosy wool-embroidered knee rug has four different
posies of flowers, each stitched in delicate shades.
The posies are then linked together with curved lines of stem
stitch and French knots.

PREPARATION

Enlarge the four posies and curved lines shown on pages 135 and 136.

Using the water-erasable pen, trace them onto the vilene. With the pen and a tape measure, mark the blanket with the positioning points for the posies and curved lines.

Following Diagram 1, find the centre of the piece of blanketing. Measure 20cm (8in) either side of the centre, down the length of the blanket. Place the top of a posy at each of these points. For the placement of the other two posies, measure 12cm (5in) either side of the centre across the width of the blanket.

Measure out 16.5cm (6½in) either side of the centre length line and 19.5cm (7¾in) either side of centre width lines.

Where these lines meet is the placement point for the middle of the curved lines, which are positioned evenly between the posies.

Baste the vilene into the correct positions using a double basting thread.

WOOL EMBROIDERY

Use two strands of wool for the embroidery except for the stems and curved line, which are worked with only one strand of wool.

Begin each thread by weaving it into the back of the blanketing for 2cm (1in). Then, make a tiny anchoring stitch before bringing the needle to the front of the work to begin the stitching.

To finish each thread, take it to the back and weave and anchor it in the same way.

While stitching each posy refer to the colour key and diagrams for colour placement. The stems in all four posies are worked in stem stitch using colour 2 wool except for the Lavender posy where

FINISHED SIZE

- 80cm x 112cm (32in x 44in)

MATERIALS

- 80cm x 112cm (32in x 44in) wool blanketing
- 140cm x 115cm (55in x 45in) wide backing fabric
- 30cm x 90cm (12in x 36in) lightweight vilene
- Appleton's Crewel Embroidery wool: one skein each of green (541, 641, 874), pink (751, 941, 942), apricot (621), yellow (871, 872, 996), blue (461, 743), lavenders (883, 884)
- Water-erasable pen
- Size 22 chenille needle
- 4.2m x 10cm (4½yd x 4in) wide satin blanket ribbon (optional)
- Tape measure
- Basting thread and needle
- Pins
- Scissors for fabric and embroidery
- Ruler
- Cardboard thread organiser

STITCHES USED

Stem Stitch, French Knots,

Satin Stitch, Straight Stitch

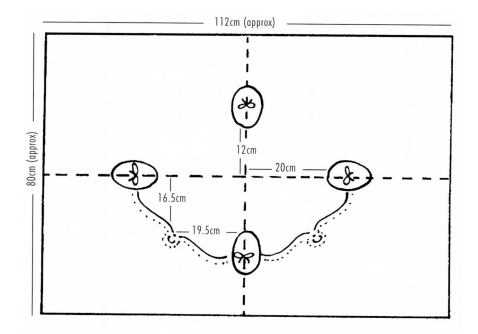

Diagram 1

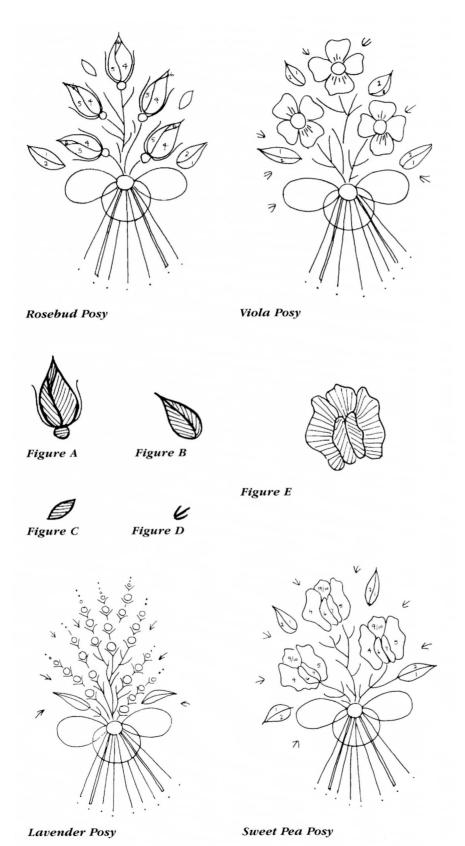

Rosebud Posy

Viola Posy

Figure A

Figure B

Figure E

Figure C

Figure D

Lavender Posy

Sweet Pea Posy

they are stitched with colour 3. The French Knots placed at the base of all the stems are worked in colour 1.

ROSEBUD POSY

The bow is also worked in Stem Stitch with the knot in Satin Stitch both in colour 5.

The circle around the stems is Stem Stitch in colour 4.

The rose petals are worked in slanted Satin Stitch in colours 4, 5 and 6 with the calyx in Stem Stitch in colour 2 and the hip in Satin Stitch with colour 1, see Figure A.

The large leaves are slanted Satin Stitch in colours 1 and 2 (see Figure B), while the small leaves are worked in slanted Satin Stitch in colour 1 (see Figure C).

Work the accent leaves with three Straight Stitches (see Figure D).

VIOLAS POSY

The bow is worked in Stem Stitch with the knot in Satin Stitch both in colour 12. The circle around the stems is Stem Stitch in colour 9.

The flower petals are worked in Satin Stitch in colour 12, with the highlights added as Straight Stitches in colour 11 and the centres filled with French Knots worked with two wraps in colours 8 and 9.

The large leaves and accent leaves are worked in the same stitches and colours as for the Rosebud posy.

SWEET PEA POSY

The bow is stitched in Stem Stitch with the knot in Satin Stitch both in colour 7. The circle around the stems is worked in Stem Stitch in colour 4.

The flowers are worked with slanted Satin Stitch in colours 4, 5, 6, 7, 9 and 10. Refer to Figure E for correct slant of stitches and the posy outline for placement of the colours.

The large leaves and accent leaves are stitched in the same stitches and colours as for the Rosebud posy.

LAVENDER POSY

For this posy, the bow is Stem-stitched with the knot in Satin Stitch both in colour 13. The circle around the stems is Stem-stitched in colour 14.

The stems of lavender are worked as groups of French Knots all worked with two wraps around the needle. Begin with the largest group at the base working six or seven knots mostly with colour 13. Make the next group four or five knots working half with colour 13 and the other half with colour 14. Then work a group with three or four knots mostly with colour 14. Finally work a group of two knots with colour 14. Add a few extra single knots in a line out from the last group using colour 14 and one wrap around the needle.

Work the Straight Stitches around each group of knots using colour 3. The large leaves are worked in slanted Satin Stitch and the accent leaves in three Straight Stitches of colour 1.

Using the water-erasable pen, trace the four posies onto the vilene before basting onto the blanket.

CURVED LINES

The curved lines are stitched using colour 1 and one strand of wool. Stitch the solid line in stem stitch then work each dot on the line above with single French Knots worked with two strands and two wraps around the needle.

REMOVING VILENE

When the embroidery is complete, remove the basting stitches. Using sharp pointed scissors, very carefully trim away the vilene from around the embroidery. Take care not to cut the embroidery threads. A pair of tweezers can also be helpful for this job.

FINISHING THE BLANKET

It is a good idea to wash the blanket before backing or binding it. Using an approved wool wash, very gently squeeze the water through the blanket. Do not rub or wring it.

Place the blanket in the machine to gently spin dry. Lay it on a towel in the shade to dry.

Placing your blanket in the sun will tend to 'yellow' pure wool blanketing.

Finish the blanket by backing it with the backing fabric.

Choose a plain or mini-floral fabric to match the embroidery.

Cut the fabric to measure exactly 20cm (8in) longer and wider than the blanket size.

Fold in and press a 5cm (2in) hem around the four sides of the backing fabric.

Fold and press again another 5cm (2in), making a double hem.

Unfold the fabric and at each corner fold in a diagonal fold and press. See Diagram 2A.

Unfold fabric and turn in the first 5cm (2in) hem. At the corners, bring the fabric right sides together along the diagonal. Sew the mitred corner as shown in Diagram 2B. This process mitres the hem as well.

Trim off the excess fabric at each corner. Press the seam open. Turn to the right side and press all hems. Place the blanket in position (see Diagram 2C) and finish by hand or machine-close to the edge. Pinning and basting carefully will help with this step.

If you wish to anchor the backing to the blanket at various places between the embroidered posies do this as invisibly as possible.

Alternatively, you can bind the edges of your blanket with satin blanket ribbon, mitring the corners for a neat finish.

Carefully remove the vilene before the embroidery is complete.

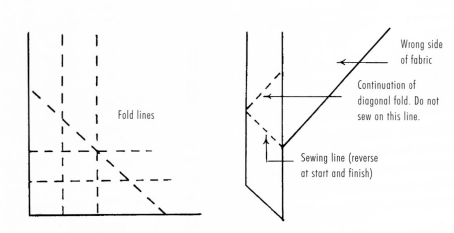

Fold lines

Wrong side of fabric

Continuation of diagonal fold. Do not sew on this line.

Sewing line (reverse at start and finish)

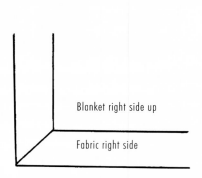

Blanket right side up

Fabric right side

Diagram 2a   *Diagram 2b*   *Diagram 2c*

SWEET PEA POSY

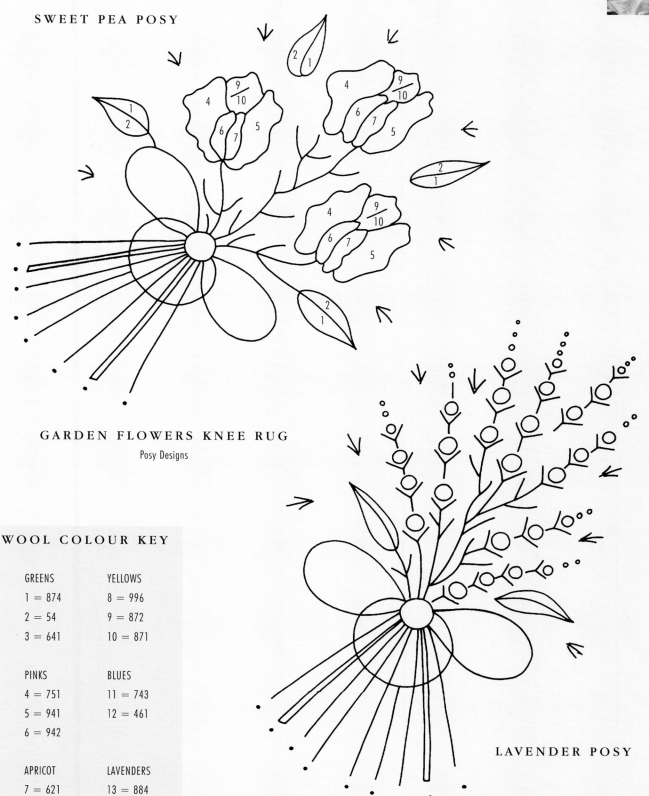

GARDEN FLOWERS KNEE RUG

Posy Designs

LAVENDER POSY

WOOL COLOUR KEY

GREENS	YELLOWS
1 = 874	8 = 996
2 = 54	9 = 872
3 = 641	10 = 871

PINKS	BLUES
4 = 751	11 = 743
5 = 941	12 = 461
6 = 942	

APRICOT	LAVENDERS
7 = 621	13 = 884
	14 = 883

107%

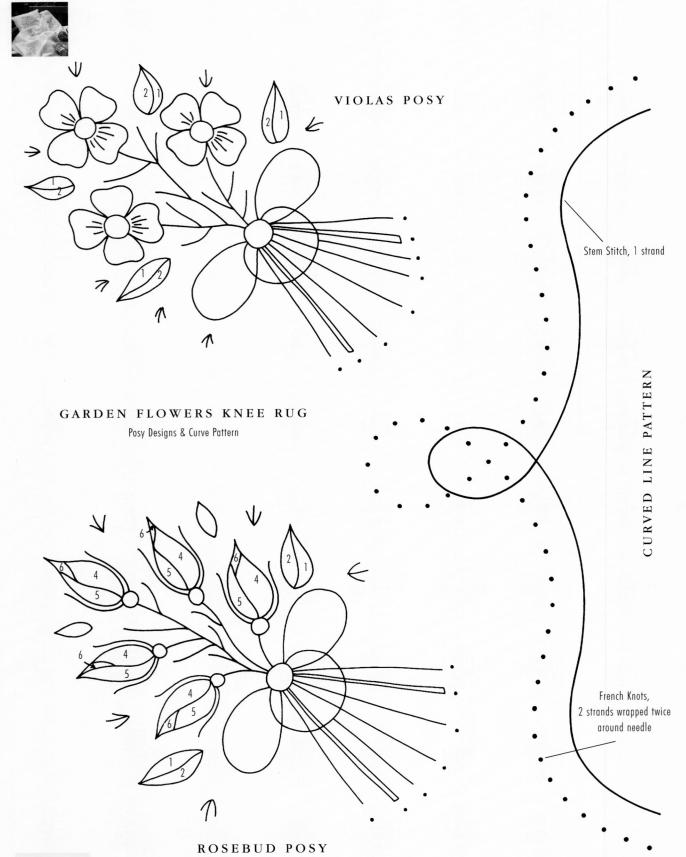

VIOLAS POSY

GARDEN FLOWERS KNEE RUG

Posy Designs & Curve Pattern

ROSEBUD POSY

Stem Stitch, 1 strand

CURVED LINE PATTERN

French Knots,
2 strands wrapped twice
around needle

107%

Beautiful Bathroom Accessories

*The elegance of a beautiful towelling bathrobe embellished with lace,
ribbon and embroidery would be a delight to have in any wardrobe.
A toiletries bag, headband and face cloth as matching accessories complement
the bathrobe. All are trimmed with Cluney lace to give a feel of real luxury.*

MATERIALS

- Towelling bathrobe
- Small bath towel to match bathrobe
- 2m x 7mm (2$\frac{1}{6}$yd x $\frac{1}{4}$in) wide satin ribbon to match bath towel
- 1m x 3mm (1yd x $\frac{1}{8}$in) wide ribbon to complement embroidery
- 75m x 5cm (27$\frac{1}{3}$yd x 2in) wide Cluney lace
- 130cm x 15mm (51in x $\frac{5}{8}$in) wide Cluney lace with elastic edge
- 70cm (27$\frac{1}{2}$in) satin piping to match bath towel
- 5cm (2in) velcro
- Sewing cotton to match bath towel
- Long crewel needle, sharp point
- DMC Coton Perlé No 3 cotton: one skein each of very light peach flesh (948), peach flesh (353), light coral (352) for roses and buds
- DMC Coton Perlé No 3 cotton: one skein each of light blue green (504), blue green (502) for stems and leaves
- Sewing machine
- Scissors, tape measure, pins

STITCHES USED

Bullion Stitch, Long Stitch, Short Stitch,
Stem Stitch, Straight Stitch

EMBROIDERING THE BATHROBE

The bathrobe purchased already had Cluney lace and ribbon around the lapels and sleeves.

Use the design outline provided on page 139 to embroider the design on the bath robe lapel using Pearl No 3 cotton and the crewel needle. The sharp-pointed needle allows for easier penetration through the thick towelling. The bullion roses are all worked with ten wraps for the centre of the roses and twelve wraps for the outside petals. The leaves are worked in Long and Short Stitch with Stem Stitch for the stems.

When the embroidery is completed tie a small bow using the 3mm ($\frac{1}{8}$in) ribbon and stitch it in place at the base of the embroidered spray.

MAKING THE TOILETRIES BAG

From the bath towel, cut a piece 35cm x 90cm (14in x 36in). Fold the towelling in half lengthwise and embroider the bullion rose design on the front of the bag, centring the design.

Use the same stitches and Perlé No 3 cotton as for the bathrobe. Finish the spray with a stitched bow in the 3mm ($\frac{1}{8}$in) ribbon.

Measure down 15cm (6in) from the top of the bag on the front and back and stitch the wide Cluney lace across the towelling with matching cotton.

Fold the bag in half right sides facing and stitch the sides with a 5mm ($\frac{1}{4}$in) seam, then overlock to neaten.

Fold down the top of the bag 7cm (3in) onto the wrong side. Stitch this wide single hem in place using a close zigzag stitch.

Measure down from the top of the toiletries bag 4cm (1$\frac{1}{2}$in) and stitch a row of straight stitching to form a casing around the bag.

Turn the bag right side out and use scissors to make slits in the top fabric layer of the casing at the side seams. Be careful not to cut all the way through the two layers of towelling.

Cut the length of 7mm ($\frac{1}{4}$in) wide satin ribbon in half and thread the ribbon through the slits in the casing, around the bag and coming out where the ribbon entered. Repeat with the other length of ribbon entering at the opposite side seam. This allows the ribbon to form a drawstring. Knot the two ends of the ribbon together.

MAKING THE HEAD BAND

From another section of the bath towel, cut a piece of towelling 65cm x 10cm (25$\frac{1}{2}$in x 4in).

Fold the towelling in half and mark the centre of the head band with a pin. Use the Perlé No 3 cotton, Bullion Stitch, Stem Stitch and Long and Short Stitch to embroider one full bullion rose in the centre of the headband and two buds at equal distances on either side. Stitch a tiny bow in 3mm ($\frac{1}{8}$in) ribbon between one bud and the main rose.

When the embroidery is complete, fold the head band over right sides facing and pin the satin piping cord in place along the long side.

Machine-stitch across one short end and along the long side, allowing a 5mm ($\frac{1}{4}$in) seam, making sure to catch in the piping cord.

Turn the head band right side out through the open end and hand stitch the opening closed. Machine-stitch the velcro at the ends of the head band.

MAKING THE FACE CLOTH

Cut a 30cm (12in) square of towelling. Use a small close zigzag stitch and machine cotton to seal the raw edges of the narrow Cluney lace, as you stitch around the edge of the face cloth.

In one corner of the face cloth embroider the design, again using Perlé No 3 cotton, Bullion Stitch, Stem Stitch and Long and Short Stitch.

Finish the headband by stitching a small 3mm (⅛in) ribbon bow on the embroidered spray.

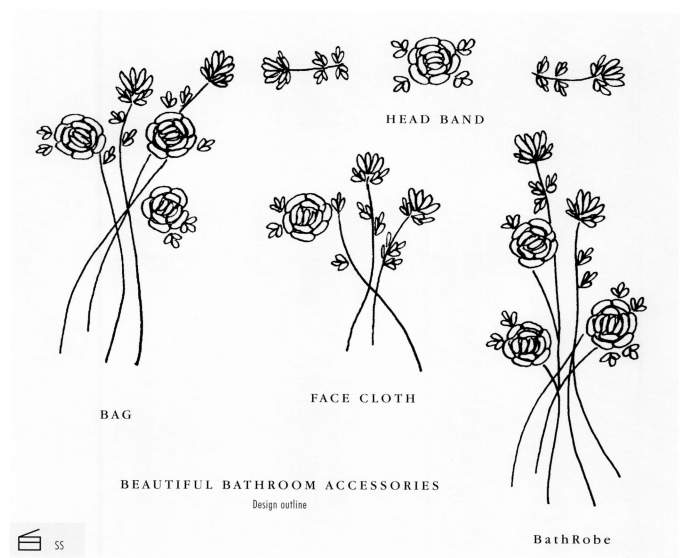

HEAD BAND

BAG

FACE CLOTH

BathRobe

BEAUTIFUL BATHROOM ACCESSORIES
Design outline

Teddy Bear Basket

Cute twin teddies, embroidered in wool, decorate the flip-up lid
that transforms a plain basket into the perfect carry-all.
A handy way to transport projects to embroidery classes, the basket
would also be ideal for outings with baby.

PREPARATION

The Pattern Sheet shows half the design, with the centre marked.

Trace the half onto greaseproof paper, transferring the centre markings. Turn the paper over and, matching the centres, draw the opposite half. Using a needle, poke a series of holes around the outlines of the bears. Also poke a hole at the centre of each large flower. Pin the tracing to the wool blanketing and press the water-erasable pen through each hole, making a dot on the fabric.

Alternatively, make holes for the large flowers only. Pin the greaseproof paper to the blanketing and mark the flower centres as before. With a double strand of contrasting machine cotton, baste around the outline of the bears.

To remove the paper without disturbing the basting, run the point of your needle firmly along the stitched lines. Then gently pull the paper apart and remove.

EMBROIDERY

The No 18 chenille needle is used throughout. You may use a smaller needle for the finer threads if you prefer.

TWIN TEDDIES

The bears are worked entirely in Alpaca wool. Embroider the outlines in whipped chain, adding the eyelashes, ear markings and claws in Straight Stitch. Satin-stitch the noses and work a Fly Stitch around the Satin-stitching to give definition. The mouths are also worked in Fly Stitch.

The bears are finished with gold necklaces and hearts. The necklace is worked in two Straight Stitches using the Goldrush thread. Stitch the heart in place using the Goldrush thread.

If you cannot fit the needle through the hole in the heart, simply unthread the needle and feed the Goldrush by hand through the hole before re-threading.

WOOL ROSES

Refer to the step-by-step directions and photograph on page 144.

Work all the roses in the following manner, using the three blue Anchor wools. The first row is worked in dark dusty blue (8740), the second row in medium dusty blue (8738) and the third row in dusty blue (8734).

Embroider the rose leaves next using Anchor deep sage (8880).

Work two Fly Stitches, one inside the other quite close together. Add a single Straight Stitch coming out from the centre of the upper Fly Stitch.

WOOL ROSEBUDS

Using dark dusty blue (8740), work a Fly Stitch (do not make the stitch too wide). Add a Straight Stitch to fit snugly in the V of the Fly Stitch, extending it slightly. Refer to the step-by-step photograph. Then embroider a Fly Stitch around the first one, using dusty blue (8734).

Split the Anchor deep sage (8880) and work a third Fly Stitch around the other two, with the holding stitch of the Fly Stitch forming the stem of the bud. Still using the deep sage wool, embroider two Straight Stitches in a V-shape at the top of your bud.

LAZY DAISY FLOWERS

Using Anchor cream (8006), embroider all the Lazy Daisy flowers, working five petals for each. At the centre of each, add a Colonial Knot using Anchor soft lemon (8036).

The leaves are worked in continuous Fly Stitch using DMC Perlé dark blue green (501).

Add a Colonial Knot at the end of each spoke of the fly stitch.

FINISHED SIZE

- 46cm x 39cm (18in x 15½in)

MATERIALS

- Approx 39cm x 33cm (15½in x 13in) strong cane basket
- 46cm x 39cm (18in x 15½in) cream wool blanketing
- 1.5m (1⅝yd) cream floral print cotton fabric
- 4m x 22mm (4⅓yd x 1in) cream double-sided satin ribbon
- Anchor tapestry wool: two skeins each of cream (8006), dusty blue (8734), deep sage (8880); one skein each of soft lemon (8036), medium dusty blue (8738), dark dusty blue (8740)
- Little Wood Fleece Mohair: one small skein each of pink/blue rainbow and dark green
- DMC Coton Perlé No 5: one skein each of dark blue green (501) and off-white (746)
- DMC Médicis wool: one skein medium beige (8308)
- Small quantity Goldrush No X2 or similar gold thread
- 2 cards Alpaca No AL70 [alternatively DMC Coton Perlé No 5 light fawn (841)]
- 4 small buttons with shank
- 1.5m x 3mm (1⅝yd x ⅛in) elastic
- 3m (3¼yd) cream or white bias binding
- Cream sewing thread
- 2.5m (2¾yd) cream gathered lace
- 3m (3¼yd) cream flat lace
- 2.5m (2¾yd) cream braid
- 2 x 46cm x 30cm (18in x 12in) sheets template plastic
- 25cm (10in) cream zip
- No 18 chenille needles
- No 9 crewel needles
- 2 tiny flat gold heart charms
- 2 pairs 9mm (⅜in) safety eyes
- Greaseproof paper, pencil
- Water-erasable pen

STITCHES USED

Whipped Chain Stitch, Straight Stitch, Satin Stitch, Fly Stitch, Lazy Daisy (Detached Chain) Stitch, Colonial Knot, Stem Stitch

NOTE: As it may not be possible to buy a basket to the same measurements as our sample, some adjustment may be necessary. If so, measure the basket opening, making sure you measure to the outside of the basket. The lid will require an overhang of 4cm (1½in) at each end of the basket and a smaller overhang of 15mm (½in) on each side. Adjust the measurements of your piece of blanketing accordingly and cut out. There will probably be only a small difference in size, but the pattern on the Pattern Sheet may require some adjustment.

VINE

The vine arching from the centre of the design above the bears is embroidered first using cream (8006) to work Colonial Knots, with a Fly Stitch around each in Coton Perlé off-white (746).

STEM STITCH ROSES

These are stitched in Little Wood Fleece pink/blue rainbow mohair. These roses are very small and may require a little practice. First, draw a 3mm (⅛in) circle with your water-erasable pen. With a double strand of the mohair, work a row of very loose Stem Stitch around the circle. Inside this circle, work another row of loose Stem Stitch. At first this may seem impossible, but it is not. To finish off the flower, just take your thread down through the centre of the rose, but leave the loop loose. End off your thread at the back of the work, being careful not to pull the loop tight.

Add the leaves in Lazy Daisy Stitch in a single strand of dark green Little Wood Fleece Mohair.

LAVENDER

Using the off-white (746) Coton Perlé, work three Lazy Daisy Stitches, then two stitches, then one stitch in the positions shown on the design. Add two Colonial Knots extending from the single Lazy Daisy. The stems are a single Straight Stitch in DMC Médicis medium beige (8308).

BEARS' EYES

Place the safety eyes in position and push the shank through the blanketing. Secure the eye by pressing the metal washer down onto the shank. Heat the blade of a knife over a flame and cut off half the length of the shank. Use the hot blade to spread the remaining plastic shank so that the washer cannot come off. An alternative to using the plastic eyes is to embroider five Colonial Knots in a tight circle using the Alpaca thread.

LINING THE BASKET

The measurements given are for the sample basket. Adjust accordingly for your basket.

Cut a paper template slightly smaller than the inside base of the basket. Pre-wash the floral print fabric.

Now cut one pattern piece using the base template.

Cut two 115cm x 33cm (45in x 13in) pieces of the floral fabric for the lining sides. Sew these two pieces together with a 2.5cm (1in) seam on the short ends, stitching 18cm (7in) from one edge and leaving the remaining part of the seam open. See Diagram 1.

Turn the unstitched section back on the seam allowance and machine- stitch as in Diagram 2. Stitch two rows of gathering stitch around the opposite edge and divide into four, leaving a pin at each point as a marker. Divide the base piece into quarters and also mark with pins.

Then overlock or oversew the non-gathered raw edge of the lining sides, starting and finishing at the openings in the seams. Hand or machine-stitch the lace around the edges, leaving the opening in the seams. Machine two buttonholes 6cm (2½in) from the lace edging and 12mm (½in) from the fold as shown in Diagram 3.

2.5cm (1in) seam allowance

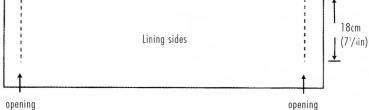

Lining sides

18cm (7¼in)

opening   opening

Diagram 1

On the wrong side of the lining sides, 5.5cm (2¼in) from the lace edge, sew on the bias binding, starting 3cm (1¼in) from the fold. Sew in two sections, one each side of the seam. See Diagram 3.

With base piece and side linings right sides together, position the seams at the centre points of the long sides of the base. Match up the quarter points and pull up the gathering to fit the base piece. Pin the lining sides around the base piece and machine-stitch in place with a 12mm (½in) seam. Overlock or oversew the edges together.

Thread a length of elastic through one of the bias binding casings. Secure at each end with a few hand stitches. Repeat for the other casing. Sew the buttons in place, 1.5cm (⅝in) from the fold.

Your lining is now complete. Place it into the basket with the base in position and the lining sides folded over the edge to the outside. Fasten the buttons to hold it in place.

LINING THE LID

❖

The lid is kept firm by template plastic inserted between the blanketing and the lining. The plastic is cut in two pieces to allow the lid flaps to open more easily.

Cut two pieces of template plastic, 10mm (⅜in) smaller all round than the pattern piece for half the lid.

Cut two lid linings from cotton fabric,

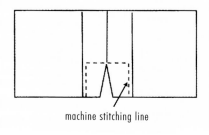

machine stitching line

Diagram 2

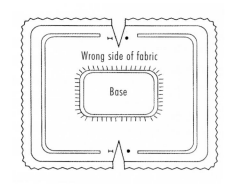

Wrong side of fabric

Base

Diagram 3

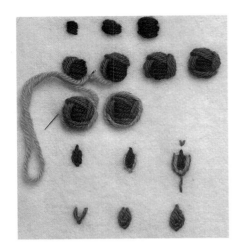

WOOL ROSES

1: Work five 4mm (1/8in) satin stitches close together.

2: Work seven satin stitches close together over the previous stitches. Make these stitches 12mm (1/2in) long, extending the stitches beyond the previous ones on one side only.

3: Bring your needle up at any corner and then take a stitch diagonally across the corner. Take the next stitch back to the same corner, but a little further over, creating a slight angle on your stitch. These two stitches are embroidered in one movement (push the needle from one point to another in one movement). At the third stitch, go straight down and turn the fabric anti-clockwise to work three stitches over the next corner. Stitch all corners.

4: To make the rose round, stem stitch in an anti-clockwise direction, keeping the stitches 12mm (1/2in) long and with the wool on top of the rose. Work two stitches past the beginning.

the same size as the pattern on the pattern sheet, but adding a seam allowance of 2.5cm (1in) at the centre of the fabric. Fold the seam allowance over to the wrong side and sew the zipper into place. You will now have a lid lining with a zipper at the centre.

Place the cotton lining and the embroidered blanketing wrong sides together. Pin all around.

To make tab closures, cut four pieces of cotton fabric 7.5cm (3in) square. Fold each piece in half with right sides facing and machine-stitch down the long side and across the short side leaving a 6mm (1/4in) seam.

Turn to the right side. On two of these tabs, sew a 1.5cm (1/2in) buttonhole, 4.5cm (2in) from the sewn edge.

Place one of the buttonholed tabs at the centre of each end of the embroidered lid. Overlock or oversew the embroidered lid and linings together. Machine or hand-stitch the lace around the edge on the right side to cover the overlocking. Hand-stitch the cream braid to the wrong side of the lid to cover overlocking.

Cut the double-sided satin ribbon into four equal pieces. With two ribbons together, sew the centre of the ribbons to the basket lid at the handle cut-out.

Open the zipper and insert the template plastic shapes. Trim to fit the shapes if necessary.

Candlewick Bolster

Candlewicking is an elegant form of embroidery that uses small knots and other basic stitches to create a raised design on fabric. It is usually worked in the same colour thread as the fabric. This charming bolster was made in cream for an antique effect.

MATERIALS

- 75cm (29¹/₂in) cream homespun fabric
- 120cm (4ft) ribbon insertion beading
- 3m x 5mm (10ft x ¹/₄in) cream satin ribbon
- 2.5m x 10cm (8ft x 4in) cream broderie anglaise lace
- 1.2m (4ft) cream bias satin piping
- Cream thread for machine stitching
- Cream candlewicking thread
- DMC Coton Perlé No 5: one skein of ecru
- No 22 tapestry needle for embroidery
- HB pencil
- 50cm (20in) cushion insert
- Large embroidery hoop (optional)

STITCHES USED

Colonial Knots, Leaf Stitch

EMBROIDERY

❖

Cut the cream homespun 48cm x 60cm (20in x 24in). Measure 7cm (3in) from the side edges and machine-stitch three pintucks 1cm (³/₈in) apart, working towards the centre of the bolster. With an HB pencil, transfer the design onto the centre of the material between the pintucks. The design is stitched using

candlewick thread for the flowers and worked in colonial knots on stalks for their centres. Leaves are worked in leaf stitch using ecru cotton. You may find it handy to use an embroidery hoop to help keep the correct tension for the stitches.

ASSEMBLY

❖

When the embroidery is complete, sew the insertion beading, threaded with ribbon, down the sides of the bolster, 5cm (2in) in from the outside edge. Sew the satin bias piping down both sides 1cm (³/₈in) in from the outside edge. Turn the bolster right sides facing and sew across the back, forming a tube shape.

Cut two pieces of homespun 12cm (5in) wide and 1.2m (4ft) long. Join the seams, press one raw edge to the wrong side 5mm (¹/₄in) and again 20mm (1in) to form a hem.

Unfold the hem edge and on the second fold line, stitch a 1cm (¹/₂in) buttonhole. Clip the buttonhole, refold the hem to the original position and sew in place along the bottom of the hem.

Cut off 125cm (50in) broderie lace and join the end to form a circle. With the stitched seam right side facing out, place the lace on the outside of the homespun. Match raw edges and run a gathering stitch around the inside edge through all thicknesses.

Gather this up to fit the outside circumference of the end section of the bolster. Sew the ends of the bolster in position 1cm (³/₈in) in from the outside edge, right sides together, making sure the piping is in the correct position. Repeat this for the other end. Roll the cushion insert into a tube shape and pull through to the inside of the bolster. Cut the remainder of the ribbon in half and insert into the ends through buttonholes and gather up tightly. Tie with a bow.

CANDLEWICK BOLSTER
Design Outline

SS

Stitch Guide

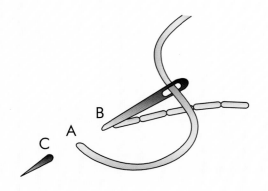

BACK STITCH

❖

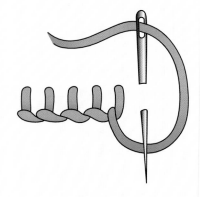

BLANKET STITCH

❖

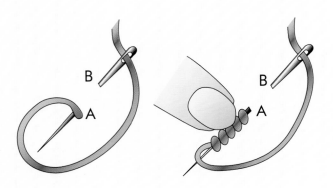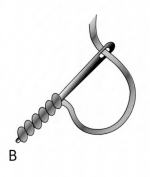

BULLION STITCH

❖

BUTTONHOLE STITCH

❖

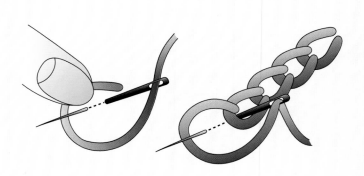

CHAIN STITCH

❖

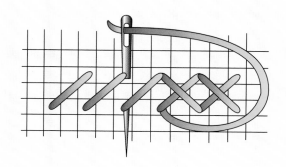

CROSS STITCH

❖

CORAL STITCH

❖

CABLE CHAIN STITCH

❖

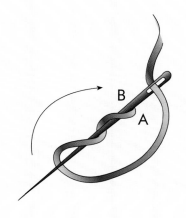

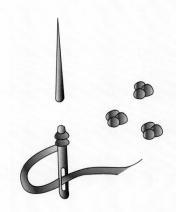

FRENCH KNOT

❖

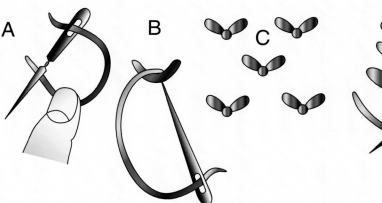

FLY STITCH

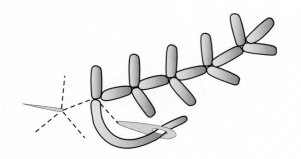

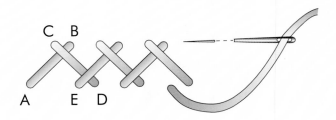

FERN STITCH

❖

HERRINGBONE STITCH

❖

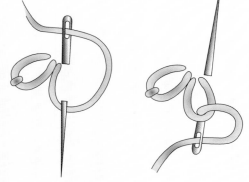

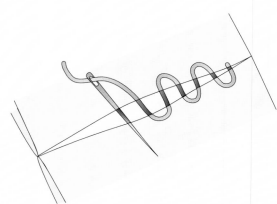

LAZY DAISY STITCH

❖

LADDER STITCH

❖

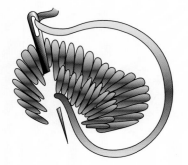

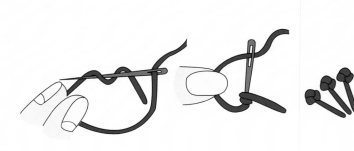

LONG AND SHORT STITCH

❖

PISTIL STITCH

❖

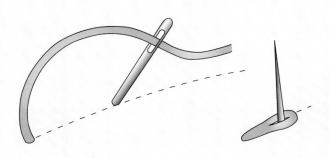

SPLIT STITCH

❖

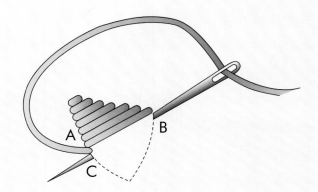

SATIN STITCH

❖

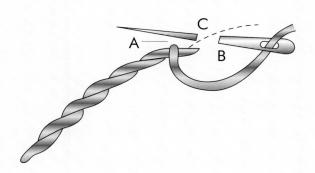

STEM STITCH: THREAD DOWN

❖

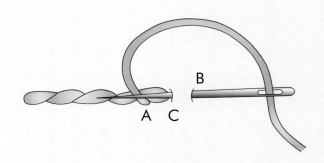

STEM STITCH: THREAD UP

❖

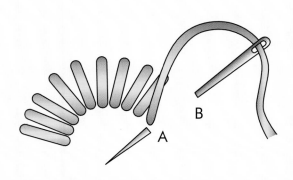

STRAIGHT STITCH

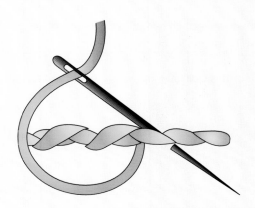

WHIPPED STEM STITCH

❖

Basic Equipment

The variety of fabric and thread suitable for embroidery is unlimited. Choice is really only determined by the type of embroidery you wish to work and the suitability of the fabric for the article to be made.

FABRIC

❖

Generally, most plain fabrics, such as linen, cottons, fine wools and a wide range of coloured furnishing fabrics, are suitable for free style embroidery. However-

er, do keep in mind that most modern furnishing fabrics come in a variety of colours, textures and finishes. They can be shiny, matt, textured or smooth. It is essential to remember that the surface and weight of the fabric must be suitable to work embroidery stitches on. Finer fabrics have more threads per centimetre and heavier fabrics have less threads per centimetre. Remember also that if you are working on sheer fabrics, the wrong side of the work will have to be kept fairly neat as it will show through on the right side.

Your choice of fabric will also govern the choice of threads you use. Always

think of the threads in relation to the material you wish to use. Consider the weight or thickness of the fabric, its texture and whether you need a matt or shiny thread, or both. Remember you do not have to use the same thread or the same thickness throughout one piece of work.

THREADS

❖

Almost any yarn or thread can be used for embroidery, just as long as it can be threaded through a needle. The variety of yarns and threads available is vast and ranges from specialist embroidery threads to ribbon, knitting and crochet yarns and even fabrics cut into fine strips.

Thread, like fabric, has a grain. If you sew with the thread going against the grain it is more likely to become twisted and tangled. When using thread off a reel, the end you pull off the reel is the end you thread through the eye of the needle and the end you cut off, is the end you knot.

Stranded Cotton or Floss

This is a very versatile and lustrous thread that is available in a full range of colours. The thread is made of six strands of cotton and any number of strands can be used depending on the effect you are trying to achieve.

Silk and Rayon Threads

Silk threads give a luxurious finish to any stitching, but are more expensive than cotton threads. Glossy rayon floss gives a similar effect.

Perlé Cotton

Perlé cotton has a high lustre finish and is spun from two plies, which are twisted to produce a beaded or 'pearl' effect. It is usually used as a single strand and comes in several thicknesses from a thick No 3 to a very thin No 12.

The most commonly used of all the Perlé cottons is the No 5 thickness and this type is also available in the greatest range of colours.

Coton á Broder

Coton á Broder has a more limited colour range than Stranded or Perlé cotton and it is also a slightly less glossy thread

Flower Thread

This is a soft-textured cotton thread with a matt finish. It is available in a wide range of colours.

SOFT EMBROIDERY COTTON

This is a relatively thick, matt-finished thread, which is used in single strands on coarse fabric.

Linen Thread

Strong and firm textured. it is not as widely available as cotton threads and comes in a limited range of colours.

Metallic Thread

These threads come in gold, silver and copper and range in thickness from very fine, to heavy cords and braids. There is a large range of metallic threads available, which can be used on their own, or mixed with to create different effects.

RIBBON

Ribbon comes in a range of widths, colours and finishes such as silk, organza, rayon and nylon. Ribbon adds another textural dimension to embroidery and is worth trying.

NEEDLES

Needles come in all sorts of shapes and sizes. They may be sharp or blunt and with a large eye or a small eye. Each sewing method requires a particular type of needle. Always use the correct type and size of needle for the particular

method you are working. If you are not sure what size needle you should be using for the number of strands of embroidery thread, compare the thickness of the needle with the thickness of the thread (they should be the same width). Embroidery needles are numbered like knitting needles. The higher the number of the needle the finer it is and the lower the number, the fatter the needle will be. The correct size needle should always be easy to thread.

Crewel Needle

These are the needles most often used for any embroidery. They have a sharp point so that they can easily pierce the fabric and a long eye to take one or more threads of stranded cotton or tapestry wool. Crewel needles come in a range of sizes from 1-10.

Straw or Milliner's Needles

A straw needle is a long, straight needle that is the same width from the top to the bottom. Straw needles range in size from the finest, a size 9, to the largest, a size 3. Straw needles are particularly good for working bullion stitches. If you have a problem when working a bullion stitch and the needle will not pull through when you have wrapped the thread around, go up a size in needles to one with a slightly bigger eye.

Tapestry Needles

A tapestry needle has a large eye and blunt point. They range in size from a large size 13 needle to a small size 26 needle. The higher the number of the needle, the smaller the needle, both becoming finer and shorter as the needle number goes up.

Chenille Needles

Chenille needles are made in the same range of sizes as tapestry needles and are similar in shape. The difference is that they have a sharp point. They have a large eye and are used for thick threads and bold stitching. They are particularly suitable for working ribbon embroidery and candlewicking

SCISSORS

❖

Good quality scissors used for the correct purpose are very important. Choose the best quality scissors that you can afford to buy. Most importantly, the scissors should be kept sharp so, if possible, buy a pair that can be unscrewed and properly sharpened from time to time.

It is also important that you use the scissors only for their intended purpose. This will ensure that they stay sharp for much longer.

Dressmaking shears have long blades and are particularly good for cutting large pieces of fabric.

Embroidery scissors have small, sharp-pointed blades which should meet smoothly and precisely. They are used for the cutting of small threads. Never use your embroidery scissors to cut paper, as this will blunt them.

Above: embroidery by Sue Strom

HOOPS AND FRAMES

❖

Hoops

If you decide to work in a hoop there is a wide range of types to choose from. Hoops hold the fabric taut, so that the stitches will lie smoothly, even after the work is released from the frame later. Hoops are made from plastic or wood and have a screw-type tension adjuster on the outside ring.

Slate or Scroll Frames

These are rectangular frames that come in a range of sizes which allow large sections to be worked on at the same time. The maximum width for your work is determined by the width of the webbing or tape attached to the rollers at the top and bottom. Any excess length is wound around the rollers at the top and bottom.

Stretcher Frames

Stretcher frames are made of wooden stretcher bars which are slotted together at the corners. Different size frames can be made by combining different size bars. Remember that the working area of a stretcher frame is the space inside the frame only.

FABRIC MARKERS

There is a whole range of fabric markers now available. Some use permanent ink, others have temporary ink which fades with water or light. Always test the marker on your fabric before using.

Transferring an Embroidery Design

There are several methods that can be used to transfer a design onto fabric, some methods are more suitable than others for specific materials or designs.

DIRECT TRACING

Probably the most simple and successful methods of transferring a pattern is to trace the design directly onto your fabric. If you are using a fairly fine or transparent fabric, then all you need to do is place your fabric right side up over the top of the design and secure in position. Trace the design onto the fabric using a fabric marking pencil or a fine lead pencil. If you are using a denser fabric, try going over the lines of the design with a black pen first, so they show up better under

the fabric. Another simple solution is to tape your design and the fabric to a window with good natural light coming through. This will help show up the design. If you intend using the tracing method a lot, you might want to invest in a light box. A light box consists of a shallow box housing a fluorescent tube and covered with opal glass.

DRESSMAKER'S CARBON

This method is probably best suited to fairly smooth-textured fabrics and is ideal for simple as well as complex designs. Dressmaker's carbon paper usually comes in packets and is available in most haberdashery departments. However, do not use office carbon paper, as this will

leave marks on the fabric. Place your fabric right side up on a firm smooth surface and secure. Place a sheet of dressmaker's carbon paper on top, with the waxed side down. Lay the design on top and secure. Using a ball-point pen or a tracing wheel and firm pressure, trace over the design.

GRAPHITE TRANSFER PAPER

Graphite transfer paper is often used by folk artists for transferring designs onto wooden pieces. It is particularly good for transferring designs onto dark fabrics because the graphite paper comes in white. It produces a fine and clear line that does not smudge and washes out. The paper is very economical because it can be used over and over again. To stop the paper tearing as you transfer the design, use a round-ended stylus for tracing.

IRON-ON TRANSFER PENCIL

There are several types of transfer pencils available on the market, some work better than others. It is advisable to test the pencil on a scrap of the fabric before using it on your embroidery. Trace the design onto tissue or tracing paper with an ordinary lead pencil.

Turn the tracing over and retrace the design on the back with the transfer pencil. Lay your piece of fabric right side up on an ironing board or heatproof surface. Place the design, with the drawn side down, onto the fabric. Using a warm dry iron (the temperature should suit the fabric) iron the back of the paper, to transfer the design onto the fabric.

WATER-SOLUBLE PEN

Trace the design onto fabric using a water-soluble pen. After stitching the design, wash the pen out in cold water.

NOTE: Do not apply direct heat (such as an iron) to the embroidery until the pen has been washed out. Heat will set the ink onto the fabric and it will not wash out.

RUNNING STITCH

This method is good for use on textured fabric. With the right side of your fabric face up, lay your traced design on top (also face up). Using ordinary thread, work small running stitches along the lines of the design, sewing through both the paper and fabric. Fasten off securely.

Gently pull off the design paper to leave the stitched design on the fabric, which can be covered with embroidery or removed as you go.

ENLARGING AND REDUCING A DESIGN

A design might not be the right size for your fabric. It can be easily enlarged or reduced on a photocopier, however if you do not have access to a photocopier then use the blocking method of enlarging or reducing a design.

To enlarge your design, enclose it within a rectangle. Make a grid of the rectangle by halving and quartering it and add further equal divisions as necessary. Cut out the rectangle and place it in the top right hand corner of a larger sheet of paper. Draw a diagonal line from the top right hand corner of the design to the

bottom left hand corner and extend the line on to the larger sheet of paper until the required height for the enlargement is reached. Draw in the horizontal and vertical lines for the new rectangle and rule in the same number of squares as in the original design. Assign matching numbers to the vertical and horizontal

lines on both grids. Copy the design from the smaller rectangle onto the larger rectangle, section by section. Make sure that each part corresponds exactly to the original.

To reduce a design, use the same method but use a smaller rectangle than the original design.

Preparing Your Work for Framing

When working a piece of embroidery with a view to framing the finished piece, there a few tips to remember.

Leave a 10cm (4in) fabric border around each side of the work to allow for plenty of options when it comes time to frame. Before you begin the embroidery, zigzag, overlock or attach fabric strips to finish the edges of the fabric.

Avoid taping as this may leave a residue and can be difficult to remove after a long period.

When working with a hoop, bind the inner hoop with white bias binding tape to prevent it from marking the fabric. When you have finished work for the day, remove the hoop and roll the fabric with right side facing the centre.

Cut any loose threads from the back of your work as they may show through when the piece is mounted. Weave the ends of a new thread under a previously worked area or leave a tail long enough to re-thread and be woven into place. Avoid knots at the ends of threads as they can pull through or form a bump.

When the embroidery is complete, wash it in lukewarm water with pure soap suds, even if it doesn't appear dirty. Don't rub, rather swish the piece around in the soapy water. Rinse under cold running water. If colour appears to run, continue rinsing until the water runs clear. Remove any excess water by placing the piece flat in the folds of a clean, white towel. Lay the work, right side down, on top of a towel and steam dry. Don't leave it to dry naturally as the threads are more likely to bleed, and never press embroidery on the right side as this flattens the stitching. Leave to thoroughly dry overnight, then press again before taking it to a framer.

The type of frame you select can completely alter the finished effect of an embroidery. As a general rule, the frame should reflect the period and style of your embroidery work.

Hang needlework away from direct sunlight and as an additional barrier against moisture, place a bumper such as a tiny round cork or small rubber suction cup on the back of the framed work. This keeps it from sitting flush with the wall and therefore allows for airflow behind it.